GOING THE DISTANCE

EXPLORING HOPE FOR AFRICAN FAMILIES IN THE DIASPORA

PEGGIE NCUBE

ZEBRON NCUBE

ISBN: 978-1-964462-95-0 (sc)
ISBN: 978-1-964462-96-7 (e)

Rev. date: 09/09/2024

CONTENTS

PREFACE

If you read the first publication of *Survival of African Families in the Diaspora*, you may be asking why you should read this *Going the Distance: Exploring Hope for African Families in the Diaspora*. Since we published the first volume, much has taken place in our society and among families. Because of that, we saw the need to broaden the scope of discussion on many of the issues that we identified in the first publication. We also felt the need to address additional issues facing African families in the diaspora, such as human sexuality and mental health, among others. Since the socio-cultural landscape is dynamic and not static, familiar issues pose new challenges, and unfamiliar issues present new threats requiring attention as they both impact the family in many ways.

We recognize the challenge of keeping pace with issues in our dynamic world, yet we must continue to shine the spotlight on new challenges to make sure that families remain strong as they are the foundation of a sustainable society. One aspect the reader will appreciate in this volume is that the table of contents shows each chapter, followed by its sub-topics for easy referencing. That way, the reader knows where to go to find a discussion on a particular issue without paging through the whole book to find it. So, welcome to *Going the Distance: Exploring Hope for African Families in the Diaspora*.

Peggie Ncube and Zebron Ncube

INTRODUCTION

T he words of J. P. De Gance engender a resounding confirmation for the necessity of this book. In a research survey on faith and relationships, he wrote:

> "Christians of all traditions must find ways to restore healthy marriages in our families, in our churches, and throughout society more broadly if the gospel can hold and again gain ground in America and across the rest of the West."[1]

Further he wrote:

> "Going beyond preaching, churches must also embrace ministry approaches that both champion and give agency to healthy relationships from youth, young adulthood, and deep into the married lie. Christian parents and churches must become serious and effective in discouraging the many existing marriage competitors (such as cohabitation) and sexual alternatives to marriage (premarital sex and pornography). . . . If pastors and church leaders fail to re-establish a cornerstone view of marriage among their people, this study demonstrates that the church

---

[1] J. P. De Gance, "Communio: Nationwide Study on Faith & Relationships," https://communio.org, accessed May 30, 2024 (p. 9).

will continue to shrink, and many more souls will be lost."[2]

The advent of *globalization* has ushered in a multitude of diverse perspectives, compelling Africans to reassess their comprehension and practice of traditional African customs. Throughout history, Africans have maintained a religious inclination, holding a cultural worldview that deems life as sacred and prohibits a strict division between the sacred and the secular. However, the influence of globalization has facilitated the proliferation of **secularization**, with Africans undergoing a transformation into adherents of this new worldview.

One of the most insidious facets of secularism is individualism, a mindset that rejects connections to one's extended family and distances itself from communal rituals and expectations in favor of pursuing personal interests. This individualistic approach gives rise to a competitive and materialistic lifestyle, eroding the communal spirit that traditionally bound African families together. Paul Peachey, in his book *Living and Clinging* (2001), observes the disappearance of the familial village, noting a shift from a molecular (communal and interdependent) to an atomic (individualistic) society. In the African diaspora, the family is compelled into survival mode.

The third wave that impacts the African family is *pluralization*. It is mainly related to the co-existence of many different cultures, ethnic groups, and belief systems. There is absolutely nothing wrong with this phenomenon per se, except that if left unchecked, it can literally wipe down one's identity. When this takes place, the African family flows with the current, in many cases, at the expense of compromising its identity and values. Consequently, the children end up shouldering the challenges of adapting to a third culture. These shifts introduce tension and strain into family dynamics, often leading to instances of separation and divorce.

The term "diaspora" is complicated to define because it carries so

---

[2] Ibid, p. 15.

many meanings with itself. The term shares meaning with big words like globalization, pluralization, and transnationalism.

According to Paul Tiyambe Zeleza, it is not always clear what people mean by African diaspora. Zeleza says that people forget that the largest African diaspora population is in Brazil and speaks Portuguese. Besides, there are several diaspora populations.[3] According to Zeleza, these are complex social, cultural, racial, ethnic, national, continental, and transnational communities.[4]

In this study, our use of the term "diaspora" comes from its historical context, which originally referred to unwilling migrations during the seventeenth and nineteenth centuries. For the purposes of this research, we narrow down the definition of the term "diaspora" to encompass groups that maintain direct ties and relations in passport countries in Africa while living in host countries outside of their own for various reasons, like educational, social, economic, or political.

It is acknowledged that many Africans in the diaspora may be married to spouses from different races who may not have direct connections with families in Africa. Additionally, in this study, "diaspora" implies the global presence of African families or individuals, suggesting their existence in various parts of the world, including the host African countries.

The book *Going the Distance: Exploring Hope for African Families in the Diaspora* addresses the impact of globalization, secularization, and pluralization on marriages and families of Africans, both in Africa and outside.

This phenomenon has resulted in the increase of fractured family relationships among African immigrants in Africa and overseas. The challenges of maintaining family bonds despite the geographical distances and cultural shifts have given rise to a complex web of emotional and social disconnection, impacting the fabric and the foundation of these families in acute ways.

However, as authors of this book, we have a firm belief that

---

[3] Paul Tiyambe Zeleza, "Rewriting the African Diaspora: Beyond the Black Atlantic," African Affairs, Vol. 104. No. 414 (Jan. 2005), pp. 35-37.
[4] Ibid., pp. 42-43.

this rapid increase in divorces, broken family ties, and conflicts in relationships can be avoided and certainly also be reversed.

This book endeavors to navigate the intricate landscape in which Africans are situated. Our sincere hope is that this book will offer encouragement to families grappling with these challenges or teetering on the brink of dissolution. Just as Jesus encouraged the church of Sardis: *"Be watchful, and strengthen the things which remain, that are ready to die. "*(Revelation 3:2). We are encouraging African families to do the same.

Jesus comprehends the struggles faced by African immigrant families; even those projecting strength may be internally shaken or traumatized by the present challenges. The comforting message from Jesus is that family ties can be restored and fortified. Instead of surrendering, families should leverage what remains, advancing to a higher level in their relationships. It's essential not to give up. Acknowledging that not every family succumbs to the challenges, some resiliently withstand the prevailing difficulties. If these families continue to push back and resist the waves, we believe they will have their names in the Book of Life (Revelation 3:5). This should be a goal set by every family. This book is a great help to that end.

God's ultimate desire is that all families should be happy, healthy, and holy. Each one of these goals is important as they play the most crucial roles in human lives. Happiness here means contentment and satisfaction rather than ecstasy and euphoria. It entails maintaining a positive outlook despite external circumstances and holding onto the broader perspective. It involves having faith in God and trusting that He is entirely in control of your life.

Desiderius Erasmus, a Dutch humanist and one of the forerunners of the Reformation, wrote a satire called *The Shipwreck*. He aimed to bring about reform from within the Catholic Church. In this satirical piece, he depicted a ship carrying church dignitaries—bishops and priests—all at sea, facing an impending tempest. Gripped by panic and fear, they fervently prayed for God's intervention. One of the prelates even promised a chest of gold in exchange for his safety. Meanwhile, others invoked the protection of Saint Christopher, Saint Peter, and Saint Mary. Amidst this turmoil, a priest noticed a woman calmly sitting in a corner, nursing her baby.

The priest inched toward the woman, thinking she was unaware of the plight that everyone was facing. The woman answered by saying, "If I pray to Saint Christopher to talk to Saint Peter to talk to Saint Mary to talk to Jesus and Jesus to talk to God, and then God sends His answer through Jesus, Mary, Peter, and finally to Saint Christopher, by that time I will have drowned. Instead, I have prayed directly to Jesus." Contentment lies in the awareness of safety amid adversity.

When we assert that God desires our well-being, it encompasses physical, emotional, and mental health. Beyond maintaining bodily and mental cleanliness, holistic health involves the overall fabric of life, encompassing attitudes, social connections, and self-perception. As beings crafted in God's image, we should possess a robust sense of identity and self-value.

To be healthy entails adhering to wholesome dietary practices, staying physically active, and ensuring a clean home environment. While we may not avert every illness, our efforts should align with honoring God and preserving the environment.

Most people pursue happiness, considering it as their top purpose in life. However, God has made it clear that holiness is His top priority for His living beings. In Matthew 4:48, Jesus calls us to holiness: *"Be ye therefore perfect, even as your Father which is in heaven is perfect"* (KJV). Also, 1 Peter 1:16 says: *"Ye shall be holy; for I am holy"* (KJV).

Christians often grapple with the concepts of "perfect" and "holy." Some associate perfection with sinlessness and view holiness as an untouchable state, suggesting an unattainable standard. The Bible employs these terms to underscore God's call for us to be distinct (saints). Our values, lifestyle, and attitudes should align with God's commandments, and we should never go against His will. It should be considered the motto of life to always do things under the shadow of God's teachings and abide by the rules set by Him till our very last breath.

When we take our relationship with God seriously, we strive to elevate it to a much deeper level. Attaining holiness or perfection is a time-consuming progression toward resembling the life and attributes of Jesus, a concept that will be explored in chapter 7 of this book.

God wants us to stay connected with Him by studying the Bible and praying every day. Holiness involves spiritual growth in our connection with God, others, and even the environment. It entails living a life that brings pleasure to God and stands out from the norm. Holiness requires the courage to embrace uniqueness. Striving for perfection means progressing spiritually and relationally in our journey with God and others.

Matthew 22:37-39 sums it up: "*Jesus said to him, 'You shall love the Lord your God with all your heart, with all your soul, and with all your mind. This is the first and great commandment. And the second is like it: 'You shall love your neighbor as yourself.'*"

We are under no illusion that family matters are complex. But because we, too, are a part of the human family, we do understand what marriage and family relationships are and how they work. What we say here presupposes that we, too, have gone through many of the issues discussed in this book in real life. So, welcome to *Going the Distance: Exploring Hope for African Families in the Diaspora*.

CHAPTER 1

FIELDS THAT IMPACT MARRIAGE

"The number one cause of divorce is marriage." Claudio Consuegra

The notion commonly expressed is that raising a child requires a village. Expanding on this idea, we can assert that comprehending and nurturing a family necessitates a collective effort from various disciplines or fields of study as well as institutions. The impact of family dynamics extends to every facet of our existence. Therefore, we dive into several disciplines and institutions crucially intertwined with what we refer to as marriage and family. Also, the survival, life, and success of marriage can be seen from the perspective of several disciplines.[5] Each of these disciplines impacts the institution of marriage and the family—"the primary cell of society."[6]

Anthropology

Anthropology is the study of humankind. It consists of two Greek words, *"anthropos"* (man) and *"logos"* (word or study of). Hence, anthropology encompasses the examination of various cultures,

---

[5] For some of these disciplines, see the list by David Olson, John DeFrain, and Linda Skogrand, *Marriages and Families: Intimacy, Diversity, and Strengths* (McGraw-Hill, NY: McGraw-Hill Humanities, 2004), p. 66.

[6] Paul Peachey, *Living and Clinging: The Human Significance of the Conjugal Unions*. Lanham Seabrook, MD: The University Press of America, 2001), p. 93.

placing an emphasis on historical perspectives to comprehend the myriad facets of the human experience. The insights derived from these studies contribute to our understanding of the extensive diversity among humans, encompassing genetics, dietary practices, health, social engagement, and communication. Henceforth, we become a more open and accepting society that appreciates diversity. The knowledge gained from anthropology also allows humans to live, communicate, and interact better, particularly in marriage and family relationships. A grasp of anthropology proves advantageous for individuals engaging in intercultural or interracial marriages. Moreover, those forming blended families for diverse reasons can enhance the quality of their familial relationships.

Child Development

Child development assists parents in providing the kind of tailored parenting and teaching skills for each stage of a child's development. As such, child development informs parents about the rites of passage or stages of a child's development. This aids parents and caregivers in addressing the requirements of children in accordance with their developmental stages.

Communication

Communication is key in sustaining every marriage relationship. Effective communication serves as the cornerstone for maintaining and nurturing every marital relationship. It forms the vital conduit through which understanding, connection, and mutual support can flourish, fostering a strong and enduring bond between partners. No marriage can make it without it. For that very reason, the quality and frequency of communication can determine the success and the failure of a marriage ultimately. In fact, if fluent communication is a part of the relationship, many problems can be resolved easily without causing any inconvenience between the two parties. More will be said later about the need for good communication skills.

Culture

Culture defines the roles expected of spouses and family members. Some may believe that embracing Christianity eliminates the need for cultural considerations. Nevertheless, shedding one's cultural identity entirely upon becoming a Christian is impractical. Culture encompasses society's shared values, thoughts, beliefs, and behavioral norms, shaping the way individuals think, feel, and behave.

Like an iceberg, culture has two layers: (1) a visible above-the-surface layer of behaviors, words, customs, and traditions, and (2) an invisible or beneath-the-surface layer consisting of worldview, values, beliefs, and language. The invisible is expressed by the visible. We often make assumptions, decisions, and judgments based on what we see without checking if what we see truly expresses what we don't see (the invisible). Appearance alone is not enough to base our conclusions on. We must go deeper to understand the motivations based on the invisible.[7] Relationships break down when values, beliefs, and worldviews clash. In other words, when values, beliefs, and worldviews collide, it presents conflicts.

Another point is that culture has a lot to do with how couples interact and behave in marriage relationships. While this is the case, it is imperative to understand that from a Christian perspective, marriage is a divine institution. Its origin is not based on culture, even though it has cultural nuances, such as negotiations leading to wedding ceremonies and celebrations.

Let us not forget that God, not humankind, established marriage. Marriage is companionship (Gen. 2:18-22), romance and sex (Gen. 2:23-24; 1 Cor. 7:1-7; Prov. 5:15-19), a covenant suggesting permanence (Matt. 19:6), joint livelihood (Prov. 31:10-31; Eph. 5:22-24), parenthood (Ex. 20:12; Eph. 6:2), and a shared religious life.[8]

---

[7] David C. Pollock, Ruth E. Van Reken, and Michael V. Pollock, *Third Culture Kids: Growing Up Among Worlds* (Boston, MA: Nicholas Brealey Publishing Hachette Book Company, 2017), pp. 56-57.

[8] Lelanf Ryken, James C. Wilhoit, Tremper Longmann III, eds. *Dictionary of Biblical Imagery* (Downers Grove, IL: InterVarsity Press, 1998), pp. 537-538.

In contemporary society, the definition of the term marriage is taking a different meaning than what God intended initially. Marriage is defined and determined by public opinion rather than by the word of God. We are now being coerced or socialized into using alternative vocabularies, such as partners instead of couples, civil union instead of marriage, or friend instead of spouse. The irony is that one is expected to be politically correct and culturally sensitive in using these expressions.

There was a period when gender (male or female) was assigned at birth, influencing traditional gender-sensitive roles within marriages. Presently, the distinctions between gender identity (male/female) and gender roles are gradually fading, giving way to more gender-neutral perspectives. The approach to marriage is evolving into a matter of personal choice and public opinion. Marriage is increasingly regarded as a civil right, framing the discourse to favor individual choices. In essence, absolutes are diminishing and yielding to a more fluid understanding.

Economy

Economic forces and finances are major contributors to stress in the family because of the current culture of materialism and consumerism.

Consequently, debt becomes a shared adversary for numerous families. Unrestrained spending facilitated by credit cards leads to consumer behavior spiraling to unprecedented levels. Addressing this requires a commitment to budgeting, financial management, and resisting the influences of media and television marketing. A grasp of economics serves as a protective barrier, shielding the family from potential financial turmoil.

Education

Education is not only about taking children to school and making sure they do their homework. This is important, but before anything, education begins at home before a child goes to a conventional school.

Home is the first school where kids begin their process of learning. Parents should teach their children values that will help them make informed decisions as they grow up and get ahead in their lives. In fact, parents must be prepared to take up this challenge, especially while children are in high school, where dating begins. Young people need to know how to choose life partners and how to remain sexually pure until marriage.

Young people need to understand that marriage is a significant commitment reserved for those who have reached a level of maturity. It goes beyond the emotional aspects and requires practical responsibilities. Financial stability plays a crucial role; having a steady job, the ability to pay rent, and supporting a family are essential components. This isn't to discourage the idea of love or companionship but rather to emphasize the importance of being prepared for the challenges that come with marriage. The foundation of a successful marriage often lies in the ability to navigate life's complexities together, with a shared sense of responsibility and readiness for the journey ahead.

Today, making children is easy, but raising them is a process that demands utmost attention and effort. It requires information, preparation, and determination. As much as children need education, parents, too, need education to acquire child-rearing skills. They must have the absolute parenting skills to raise their children in the right way. Nothing should be left to chance.

Human Biology

Furthermore, an understanding of human biology not only enhances our comprehension of physiological processes but also cultivates an awareness of the intricate interplay between genetics, environment, and lifestyle. This holistic perspective aids in making informed choices that contribute not only to individual well-being but also to the dynamics of interpersonal connections, reinforcing the foundation for robust and enduring relationships. An understanding of human biology helps us deal with childhood years, teenage years, middle age issues, old age, and other crises that so often affect intimacy in marriage relationships.

Law

Many individuals tend to underestimate the impact of the law on marriage and family life. The choice to enter matrimony invokes the legal regulations of the state or country where the marriage is formalized. For instance, even though we were originally from Zimbabwe, we got married in Michigan, USA. We had to comply with the laws of marriage in the State of Michigan.

While a marriage from each state or country is recognized by every country in the world, the laws governing the behavior and relationships in families differ. For example, some African countries have laws that approve the practice of polygamy, while other countries reject such a practice.

Laws of marriage in one country are different from those of another. In South Africa in 1998, the Government passed The Recognition of Customary Marriage Act (12). This customary law applied to "indigenous African peoples of South Africa, which form part of the culture of those people."[9] This law did not recognize Islamic and Hindu marriages that took place in South Africa. They had to continue to be unrecorded for the foreseeable future. Also, in Malawi, the government and the church recognize *Chinkoswe*—a traditional marriage that is the result of the agreement between the two families after and when lobola (bride price) has been agreed to. Chinkoswe is a public celebration that even pastors sometimes attend as part of the community. This is sometimes extended to *Chinkoswe Chotengeracho*—a traditional marriage followed by a church wedding.[10]

Laws pertaining to the ownership of property by married couples

---

[9] Debbie Bundlender, Ntobelang Chobokoane and Sandile Simelane, "Marriage patterns in South Africa: Methodological and substantive issues," Southern African Journal of Demography, Vol. 9, No. 1 (June 2004), p.3.

[10] Curtesy of Dr. Saustin Mfune, retired General Conference of Seventh-day Adventists Children Ministry associate leader, now residing in Malawi.

vary across countries. In numerous African nations, the customary practice of paying a bride price, commonly known as lobola in Zulu and Ndebele, persists, although its observance may be optional in some jurisdictions. Regardless of where a marriage is solemnized, couples are obligated to adhere to the legal frameworks of their residing countries or states.

For instance, if a couple weds in Africa but resides in the United Kingdom, the laws governing marital relations in the United Kingdom take precedence. Certain cultures recognize cohabitation for a specific duration as constituting marriage (common law marriage). However, this doesn't imply that couples cannot uphold African values and traditions in their new residence, especially when maintaining connections with relatives in Africa. It is crucial for them to remain culturally relevant in the African context.

Nevertheless, there may be instances where cultural practices conflict with the laws of the host country. In such cases, the laws of the host country supersede cultural traditions. For example, the customary practice of paying lobola, while culturally significant in one's home country, cannot be enforced among families residing in the United Kingdom. The accommodation of personal religious preferences and practices is generally upheld wherever the family chooses to reside.

Literature

Literature about family and marriage is unlimited. It shapes the way individuals, couples, and families think and relate to issues that affect their lives. Exploring the stories and experiences of others expands one's perspective and enhances the ability to navigate personal situations with greater insight and clarity.

Reflecting on one's family history establishes the groundwork for a familial viewpoint and fosters an appreciation for the family's heritage. Examining family history not only lays the foundation for a family perspective and appreciation of heritage but also enables a connection with past traditions, fostering a sense of identity. Literature plays a vital role in aiding families in navigating contemporary challenges, while historical insights prevent the repetition of past mistakes.

Medicine

Medical and health professions are familiar entities to every person. Families are frequently involved with medical and health professionals, as every stage of life needs health professionals. Marital relationships intersect with the realm of medical and health professions, making self-disclosure a crucial aspect for married individuals. In certain countries, pre-marital medical examinations are mandatory. Despite privacy considerations, maintaining transparency between spouses regarding health matters is paramount, potentially serving as a lifesaving practice. Failure to share information with your spouse can put the relationship at risk, and unfortunately, it can even be a cause of death.

Psychology

The study of psychology aids in comprehending the human mind and behaviors. In the context of marital challenges, fields such as counseling psychology, clinical psychology, family psychology, and social work offer valuable insights and assistance in addressing issues within marriages and families. Couples facing difficulties should be open to exploring these disciplines for guidance.

Sociology

Sociology contributes to the comprehension of social interactions, delving into the intricacies of everyday culture, human structures, and relationships. When examining marriage, sociologists view it as a social institution intertwined with legal, economic, and religious dimensions. Consequently, factors influencing marriage often manifest within these realms of family life.

Human Sexuality

The understanding of marriage and family perspectives is influenced by the concept of human sexuality. This involves how individuals interpret, undergo, and articulate their sexual experiences, considering biological, physical, emotional, social, and spiritual aspects of feelings and behaviors. We recognize that this is a hot-button issue today due to the phenomenon of the alphabet communities, the LGBTQIA+ (lesbian, gay, bisexual, transgender, queer, intersex, asexual, plus). Mary Eberstadt calls this the "sexual revolution," to which "people must agree to disagree."[11]

Debate on these issues is endless. For example, proponents of homosexuality look at opposition to homosexuality as discrimination because "it is defined by the majority as different and, therefore, deviant."[12] According to D. Stanley Eitzen and Maxine Baca Zinn, "Societies create right and wrong by originating norms and saying that failure to follow the rules constitutes deviance."[13]

In other words, they argue that "deviance" (or abnormality) is not necessarily inherent in the behavior itself, but it is conferred upon by those who see the behavior. In other words, sexuality is both a biological and social construction. Society shapes our ideas about what is erotic, taboo, and "who are appropriate sexual partners."[14] Consequently, there is a movement advocating for gender-neutral marriages (unions), language, clothing, amenities, and documentation in form-filling. The inherently complex nature of sexuality has sparked conflicts, impacting us physically, emotionally, socially, politically, and spiritually.

Nicholas P. Miller, a lawyer and church historian, in his book, *500*

---

[11] Mary Eberstadt, *It's Dangerous to Believe: Religious Freedom and Its Enemies* (New York: Harper, 2016), p. 103.

[12] D. Stanley Eitzen and Maxine Baca Zinn, *Social Problems*, 10th ed. (Boston, MA: Allyn and Bacon, 2006), p. 285.

[13] Ibid.

[14] Ibid.

Years of Protest and Liberty, discussed gay marriages at a time when the USA Supreme Court was to vote on whether to legalize and recognize the practice. He wrote:

> But once gay marriage is recognized, there will be a legal presumption, and increasingly a popular assumption, that these are fully adequate child-rearing environments. Society will assume that little boys can grow into well-rounded men without the benefit of masculine influence; that little girls can become mature women without feminine nurture and guidance.
>
> This is an unsafe and even foolish assumption that goes against the common experiences of those raised by a mother and a father, most who cannot imagine choosing between them. It also goes against the experience of those raised by single parents and who feel very deeply the lack of the "other" parent in their lives. Increasingly, children raised by gay parents are expressing their unhappiness at the lack of, usually, a father figure.[15]

Miller also observed the tendency of pitting religious freedom against equality (a gay mantra). He quoted Milton Friedman, who once said: "The society that puts equality before freedom will end up with neither. The society that puts freedom before equality will end up with a great measure of both." Miller concluded: "To renege on our founding promise of religious freedom and to try to fight 'religious bigotry' with the new regime of a secular egalitarianism will lead to a new and more intensive kind of bigotry—one toward religion and religious people. This is the true new bigotry."[16]

Undoubtedly, human sexuality presents a challenge, particularly

---

[15] Nicholas P. Miller, *500 Years of Protest and Liberty: From Martin Luther to Modern Civil Rights* (Idaho: Pacific Press Publishing Association, 2017), p. 181.
[16] Ibid., p. 178.

for Bible-believing Christians, as it often conflicts with the norms of postmodern society. The Seventh-day Adventist World Church, in response, formally addressed transgenderism in a statement dated April 11, 2017. The statement defines transgenderism as "gender dysphoria," encompassing the physical and emotional aspects of individuals whose gender identity differs from their biological sex.

This declaration provides a comprehensive understanding of transgender conditions, offering nuanced insights. The Church's stance encourages individuals experiencing incongruity between biological sex and gender identity to approach their distress in accordance with biblical principles. Unfortunately, public discussions about human sexuality often exclude the authority of Scripture.

Human sexuality extends beyond theological debates to the pursuit of sexual fulfillment, not only within marriages but also among those who perceive it as a fundamental physical and social need, irrespective of marital status. The market for products catering to sexual satisfaction reflects the significant demand, leading to health concerns such as sexually transmitted diseases. Society frames sexuality as a civil rights issue, advocating against discrimination based on sexual orientation.

The church finds itself entangled in broader gender discussions, including women's ordination and same-sex marriages. Sexuality, unlike other topics, invokes cultural, political, legal, philosophical, moral, ethical, and religious dimensions. The biblical perspective underscores marriage as a divinely ordained heterosexual relationship, emphasizing that sex should be certified, sanctified, and exclusively between a man and a woman.

St. Augustine (354-430 AD), Bishop of Hippo in North Africa, is credited with laying the foundation of Western theological thought. One of the theological positions he formulated dealt with human sexuality. Earlier in his life, he confronted the Manichaeans, a religious group of Persian origin. This group believed and taught that having sex was bad and that having children was a crime. Augustine's views on sex reflected his revulsion against the Manichaean avoidance of procreation, which, in his view, was the primary purpose of marriage.

According to Augustine, it was a sin to have sex without having children in mind.[17]

It is crucial to acknowledge that St. Augustine, an African theologian, provided a theological perspective on human sexuality within the context of marriage in the mid-fifth century. Over time, the discourse on this subject has evolved, acquiring numerous facets and dimensions. However, the primary focus of this book is to examine both the Biblical and African perspectives on marriage.

Biblical and African Worldviews

Genesis 1:27-28 is the very first biblical text giving us a perspective on marriage: "*So God created man in His own image; in the image of God He created him; male and female He created them. Then God blessed them, and God said to them, Be fruitful and multiply; fill the earth and subdue it. . .*" (*NKJV*). Three significant facts are highlighted here. Firstly, the creation of man and woman in God's image endowed them with the ability to communicate with both their Creator and each other, establishing communication as a foundational principle in their relationship. Secondly, the inherent gender differences between males and females are acknowledged. Thirdly, the divine instruction to "be fruitful and multiply" underscores the aspect of procreation. These three facts are intricately interwoven, shaping the fundamental aspects of human relationships. Communication, procreation, and gender are factors in marriage. For procreation to occur, there must be a male-female sexual relationship. This was the only science lab for procreation given to Adam and Eve.

In Genesis 2:18, "helper" is used to refer to Eve. Many English translations wrongly translate the Hebrew word "*ezer*" to suggest that Eve was created as Adam's assistant. The word in Hebrew can be translated as "power" and "strength." This means Eve was equal to

---

[17] Roland H. Bainton, Christendom: A Short History of Christianity and Its Impact on Western Civilization, Vol. 1 (New York: Harper & Row Publishers, 1966), p. 130.

Adam and fully his match. She brought strength and power to Adam, who was struggling with aloneness.[18]

In Genesis 2:23, God created Eve and gave her to Adam. *"And Adam said: 'This is now bone of my bones and flesh of my flesh; She shall be called Woman, because she was taken out of Man"* (NKJV). This can be considered Adam's poetic expression of gratitude. While the English language often refers to blood relationships, the Hebrew language emphasizes connections of flesh and bone. Therefore, *"bone of my bone and flesh of my flesh"* is a covenant—a declaration of kinship relationship. It identifies the two as uniquely each other's bones and distinguishes them from animals. It sets the two apart from the rest of the creatures. This thought is also expressed in Song of Solomon 2:16: *"My beloved is mine, and I am his"* (NKJV).

The Hebrew expression, *"she shall be called woman,"* is a pronouncement that a father makes at the birth of a child. The naming seems to indicate man's participation in the creative process with God. In Hebrew, *ish* (man) and *ishshah* (woman) emphasize the similarity of both being human but sexually different for the purpose of procreation.[19] This underscores the significance of human identity and the complementarity of both genders. Marriage serves as a reunion of individuals already united by their shared humanity. Thus, marriage is inherently a bond between sexually different human beings, specifically between man and woman.

What follows is God's declaration: *"Therefore a man shall leave his father and mother and be joined to his wife, and they shall become one flesh. And they were both naked, the man and his wife, and were not ashamed"* (Gen. 2:24-25 NKJV). Paul Peachey rightly states: *"Leaving* parents to *cling* to a spouse represents the threshold into maturity and autonomy in the individual course of life."[20] Peachey tells the story of an old legend

---

[18] Walter C. Kaiser Jr., Peter H. Davids, F. F. Bruce, Manfred T. Brauch, *Hard Sayings of the Bible* (Downers Grove, IL: InterVarsity Press, 1996), p. 94.
[19] Bill T. Arnold, *Genesis: The New Cambridge Bible Commentary* (New York: Cambridge University Press, 2009), p. 60.
[20] Paul Peachey, *Leaving and Cleaving*, p. 93. Italics not supplied.

about Adam bringing Eve back to God and complaining, "I can't get along with her, and I can't get along without her."

The concept of a man leaving his parents implies independence in providing for his wife. In patriarchal Bible-era cultures and many African rural communities today, men often stay close to their parents. This dynamic means that women leave their parents to join the man's family. The term "cleave" emphasizes an enduring emotional connection, indicating a lasting passion. "Forsake" and "cleave" signify a permanent covenant, altering priorities and obligations in marriage.

Several texts in the Bible help us frame a balanced perspective towards what family relationships should be, especially the relationships between spouses. The highest goal in life is that Christ should be exalted (magnified) in our bodies (Phil. 1:20). We should do everything to glorify Christ. He owns our bodies (1Co 6:19, 20); so, do spouses own each other's body (1Co 7:4; Eph 5:28). However, that being the case, the Apostle Paul reminds us that each person must discipline his or her own body, not the other person's (1Cor 9:27). Giving your body to the other person without love does not profit you (1Cor 13:3). This text rebukes all situations of sexual or social abuse and respects one's freedom of choice.

Paul in Ephesians 3:17-19 appeals to Christians to strive to know the love of Christ—its width, length, depth, and breath—"which passes knowledge." While this focuses on the Divine-human relationship, it also speaks to human-human relationships. Love is never fully fathomed or fully comprehended. In a marriage setting, love continues to grow deeper, wider, broader, and longer. In Romans 13:8, Paul says love is a debt we can never fully pay off. Therefore, spouses should explore such love in the context of their relationship.

Going back to Genesis 2, Adam and Eve were naked and did not have a sense of shame. This says more than just nudity. Transparency and openness between them were the fundamental building blocks of their marriage. Thus, good communication in marriage depends on men and women being open with each other. There should be no cover-ups between married people. They should be open and willing to share their inner dynamics—thoughts and feelings. Marriage, not sex, is the only means designed by God for establishing a family. It is the gateway to sexual union. The family, through marriage, is the cornerstone that establishes a society and a nation. William Hendriksen states: "No institution on earth is more sacred than that of the family. None is more basic."[21]

Barring wider society's definitions of marriage, the Biblical perspective on marriage continues to be the basis of the marriage union. Yet, with the formation of states, countries, and continents, marriage incorporates legal dimensions governed by the established laws of the respective state or country where the couple decides to solemnize it. Any marriage conducted outside legal regulations is akin to a house built on shifting sands. Among other things, society depends on marriage and family for stability and happiness. In fact, the home carries the weight of the world on its shoulders. When the family fabric falls apart, the rest of society goes down with it. When families are strong, society is strong.

Marriage and the family are profoundly influenced by various fields of study and institutions, rendering them multidisciplinary entities. From the moment a couple chooses to marry, numerous disciplines come into play, highlighting that marriage is intricately connected to and shaped by a range of diverse influences.

It is important to look at how marriage is generally understood in Africa. For the most part, marriage has a communal perspective and meaning. It is founded on the basic cultural value of community or communalism. This is better explained by an African saying: "*The prosperity of a single person does not make a town rich. But the prosperity of the town makes persons rich.*"[22] Aylward Shorter observes that "in East Africa, as in other parts of Africa, the family group is seen as logically prior to the institution of marriage . . . The family is seen,

---

[21] William Hendriksen, New Testament Commentary: Galatians, Ephesians, Philippians, Colossians, and Philemon (Grand Rapids, MI: Baker Books, 2004), p. 248.
[22] Oliver A. Onwubiko, *African Thought, Religion & Culture* (Enugu, Nigeria: Bigard Memorial Seminary, 1991), p. 15.

nevertheless, as a pre-existing entity."[23] This means that marriage finds its meaning in the larger family. Aylward Shorter further states that the family is a community. Even though people did not share a common residence, families exercised a certain amount of mutual co-responsibility in family affairs, such as inheritance, marriage, and education of children.[24]

Daniela Berghahn defines the family as "a social group characterized by common residence, economic cooperation, and reproduction. It includes adults of both sexes, at least two of whom maintain a socially approved sexual relationship, and one or more children, owned or adopted, of the sexually cohabiting adults."[25] This definition of what constitutes family, though general, is quite comprehensive.

From an African perspective, when a man and a woman get married, their families and communities begin a kinship relationship. Marriage unites people, communities, and nationalities that are friendly or unfriendly to each other. They bind them together as a whole. We see this unifying concept of marriage even in Bible times and in later centuries. Kings had diplomatic marriages to build alliances and bring about unity and peace. For example, in Daniel 11:6, the king of the north (Syria) and the king of the south (Egypt) were at war against each other. The marriage of Bernice (of Egypt) to Antiochus II Theos (of Syria) was an attempt to bring about peace.[26]

The connection between spouses extends to the bonding of groups, communities, and nationalities. Essentially, when entering marriage, you bring your community with you into the relationship; it's not a solitary journey. The people from your origin become intertwined with the people of the region you are marrying into. Marriage holds the

---

[23] Aylward Shorter, *East African societies* (London: Routledge & Kegan Paul, 1974), p. 67.

[24] Ibid.

[25] Daniela Berghahn, *Far-Flung Families in Film: The Diasporic Families in Contemporary European Cinema* (Edinburgh University Press, 2013), p. 19.

[26] William H. Shea, *The Abundant Life Bible Amplifier, Daniel 7-12*, edited by George R. Knight (Boise, Idaho: Pacific Press Publishing Association, 1996), p.182.

transformative power to mitigate differences and potential conflicts among diverse communities.

It is unheard of in Africa to have a marriage ceremony without the participation or representation of parents or families from both sides. Johan de Smedt describes the child marriages in Rwandan refugee camps in Tanzania where girls 13-14 years old were getting married to boys 14-15 years old. Sadly, many of these marriages didn't last; the boys would send their wives away. His observation was that communities were concerned about the loss of the Rwandan culture and traditional values. In Rwandan culture, marriage was used to strengthen the lineage or family's position. For that reason, one had to choose well, and such a choice was not to be left to boys to make—the very thing that was being done in the refugee camps. One of the values lost in these child marriages was the payment of the gift (*indongoranyo*) to the family.[27]

In Africa, marriage is a communal affair characterized by a deliberate, prolonged, and intricate process aimed at ensuring adherence to cultural norms and establishing safeguards for the well-being of both parties involved. When separation or divorce transpires, its impact resonates throughout the community, extending beyond the married couple. Despite evolving societal norms, the communal essence of marriage persists, subjecting couples to the challenge of adapting their roles to societal shifts. This adjustment, however, often leaves lasting scars on marital relationships, as change disrupts established equilibrium, and people tend to find comfort in familiar traditions.

APPLICATION: Which fields or disciplines do you feel have the most or less impact in shaping your relationship? Why?

---

[27] Johan de Smedt, "Child Marriages in Rwandan Refugee Camps", Africa Journal of the International African Institute, Vol. 68, No. 2 (1998), p. 211.

Chapter 2

CHALLENGES IN FAMILY RELATIONSHIPS

"The need to remain right about people, places, and religion always sacrifices intimacy." Ron Rockey

For many years in pastoral ministry, both in Africa and in North America, we have worked closely with families and couples to restore hope in family relationships. After having a broad experience of working with families with broken relationships, we have concluded that family challenges are many and diverse. They can be of any sort. Most of these challenges are very little in the beginning but are enough to trigger a big feud that can result in arguments, which can lead to separation in the family. We do not claim to enumerate all of them but will highlight the most common challenges that tear up relationships today. Further discussion and solutions to these challenges will be addressed and discussed in detail later.

Communication

The bedrock of every family relationship is communication. Many years ago, before Peggie and I (Zebron) were in a love relationship, we used to write each other letters back and forth. These written expressions were the seeds that blossomed into the deep-rooted love we share today. Over the years, our commitment to open and heartfelt communication has fortified the bedrock of our relationship, fostering understanding and strengthening the ties that bind us together. In those early days, as we penned our thoughts and emotions, little did we know that we were sowing the seeds of a lasting and resilient love story that would stand the test of time.

One day she wrote me a letter to tell me she had fallen in love with me. I read that letter many times over with excitement. She lived in a town two hours away from where I was working. After the dust had settled in my mind, I began asking myself, "now that she has fallen in love with me, what am I going to say the first time I meet her?" In my nervousness, I began jotting down some thoughts and ideas. Sad to say, it all vanished once I met her in person. It was like a cartoon about a chimpanzee that sat down after a test, and with hands over its head, it said: "When I thought I had all the answers, they changed the questions."

After more than four decades of marriage, we continue to find an abundance of topics to discuss and activities to enjoy together. The flow of conversation and shared experiences happens effortlessly; there's no need for a daily agenda. Our sense of security stems from the profound trust we have in each other. Trust is the cornerstone of safety in our relationship; where trust is absent, so is a feeling of security. Love serves as the solid foundation for all familial connections, binding us together through the years. In 1 John 1:18, it says, "there is no fear in love."

In Latin the word "communicate" means to make common or to share. It is a process of understanding and sharing meanings. To say it differently, communication is the process of meaning-making. This means being a participant in an activity, exchange, or behavior.[28] Communication is an ongoing and dynamic process, constantly evolving over time. It improves with the passage of time, embodying the capacity and readiness to articulate thoughts, emotions, and aspirations through both verbal and non-verbal means. This encompasses not only

---

[28] Judy C. Pearson and Paul E. Nelson, An Introduction to Human Communication, 8th ed. (Boston: McGraw Hill, n.d.), P. 5; Lynn H. Turner & Richard West, Perspectives on Family Communication, 2nd ed. (Boston: McGraw Hill, 2000), p. 14.

the skill but also the willingness to actively listen and understanding the messages your partner endeavors to convey.

The term "endeavor" is employed because individuals may not always possess the precise words and methods to thoroughly convey their thoughts and emotions. The efficacy of marital relationships hinges on the way couples communicate, determining success or failure based on the effectiveness of their communication. If they improve the quality of communication, relationships will also improve. Nearly every marital challenge contains an aspect of communication as part of its solution. In essence, adept communication practices form the foundation of relationship building. This involves the ability to navigate digital media communication, including platforms like Instagram, Twitter, texting, and various chat platforms.

Intimate Violence

Many of us have had a friend or neighbor show up with a black eye or report that they were verbally or physically abused. Present in contemporary families, intimate violence, commonly known as domestic violence, poses a significant challenge. Manifesting in diverse forms, it includes acts of physical violence, exposure to inter-parental violence, coercive behavior, emotional abuse, harm to pets, economic dependency leading to isolation, property destruction, and verbal abuse. While a lot is said about women and children as victims, men are also abused. Due to the gravity and complexity of this matter, Chapter 7 has been specifically devoted to addressing this issue.

Conflict

Somebody once said conflict is not necessarily a problem; combat is the problem. It is a fact that every family is, to some extent, dysfunctional. As the proximity in a relationship increases, so does the likelihood of unintentionally causing discomfort. Intimacy and familial ties bring forth numerous expectations, assumptions, and things taken for granted. Consequently, the personal affairs of each individual start to become a collective responsibility and, paradoxically, nobody's specific responsibility. Conflict happens to people with common interests when each side feels it might lose. In that sense, conflict becomes a function of caring.

In the context of African marriages, characterized by communal and extended family structures, conflicts often take on a multifaceted nature. Disputes between couples have the propensity to rapidly diffuse and intensify, encompassing other branches of the family tree, including in-laws and relatives. Once this happens, managing or resolving the conflict can prove to be a nightmare. It's like spaghetti; you don't know where to begin or end. Anyone who tries to jump in to resolve the concerns may end up becoming part of the problem. Hence, it becomes crucial for the couple to grasp the dynamics of conflict, acquiring essential skills to navigate and manage conflicts effectively. This approach is integral to achieving a relationship that is not only joyous and robust but also characterized by a sense of sacredness.

Spirituality and Family Worship

We live in a world where everybody seems to be hard-pressed for time. The rapid pace of our lives often poses a challenge to maintaining a sustainable connection with God, family, and the church. This struggle is particularly pronounced among African families living in the diaspora, who can attest to the complexities of balancing these essential facets of life. Every member of the family is in a rush to meet the next appointment, that is, getting kids ready for school, rushing to work, taking kids for extra curricula activities such as sports, music lessons, etc., only to come home for a short time and then move on to the next job.

In the diaspora, family togetherness during meals or bedtime is a rarity for many. Weekends, instead of providing respite, are often consumed by additional work to supplement income for home mortgages, student loans, and car loans. Any available free time is frequently utilized for much-needed rest and catching up on sleep. Because of busy schedules, personal and family devotions, parenting, and quality time with kids, affection, intimacy and romance, conversation, recreational companionship, entertainment, and sexual fulfillment are compromised. Life is like a freight train racing toward self-destruction.

Money Matters

Through extensive conversations with families, it becomes evident that financial issues are a pivotal source of conflicts, often ranking at the forefront of contentious areas. Surprisingly, it is not always the scarcity of funds but rather how finances are handled that impacts marital relationships. Cherie and Brian Lowe, featured on the radio program "Focus on the Family," highlighted that engaging in weekly money-related conflicts increases the likelihood of divorce by approximately 30 percent.

How money matters are handled in a relationship can destroy trust. We have found that too many financial conflicts are a result of competing goals in the family, more so the families in the diaspora. Because of very limited resources, immigrants tend to compete for opportunities. The pursuit of individual success, irrespective of its impact on the family, can strain relationships significantly. Such a mindset often neglects the collective well-being. That's why the establishment of sustainable goals and budgets is crucial to fostering harmony within the family unit.

Coping with Change

In biology, we learn that old cells in our bodies are replaced by new ones at the rate of millions per second. Besides, a cell goes through different stages or divisions. Indeed, the only constant is change. Those resistant to change, irrespective of its nature, are setting themselves up for familial challenges. Embracing change is pivotal for navigating the evolving dynamics within a family successfully.

Because change is inevitable, it behooves us to learn how to adjust or adapt as the situation requires. For example, those of us in the diaspora who traveled 20-25 hours by air from Africa had to deal with jet lag upon arrival in America. Our bodies underwent adjustments to diverse time zones, varying weather patterns, unfamiliar foods, distinct language accents, and numerous other factors. Even our family rhythms changed—having two or three jobs and going to school at the same time, fathers having to cook and do dishes, and mothers becoming bread winners so husbands could go to school.

Changes extend to different aspects, including stages of development, aging, retirement, joblessness, geographical locations, cross-cultural contexts, marital status, and experiences of loss or death. Like the body adapting to weather and time zones, acknowledging the inevitability of change and being flexible to make required adjustments is essential. Coping with change is imperative for the survival of any marriage.

One big area of change that is plaguing African families in the diaspora is the disappearance of the distinctive roles between husband and wife. In the past, a wife was known to be dependent on her husband. She was always beholding to her husband, who provided everything and made decisions based on the power of that role. Today, things have changed. The widespread professionalism and financial independence of women introduce a dynamic that can lead to tension between spouses, often escalating to divorce. Navigating this reality poses a threat to established cultural norms, and regrettably, for many, divorce is seen as the necessary course of action.

Unwillingness to Forgive

Bishop Desmond Tutu's well-known statement nailed it on the head when he said, "There's no future without forgiveness." Three misconceptions about forgiveness require our attention. Firstly, forgiveness is occasionally misconstrued as a diplomatic gesture enabling people to move forward, indicating a lack of comprehension of its true nature and process. The question of whether the victim, the perpetrator, or both should extend forgiveness can lead to confusion, contributing to ongoing conflicts when the act of forgiveness is not fully understood.

The second misconception about forgiveness is that some people find forgiveness to be a painful experience to go through. How do you forgive someone who caused you so much pain? Should you forgive that person? When Jesus said we should love our enemies and do good to those who persecute us, this was and is radical thinking some find not practical. Forgiveness should not be a painful endeavor, for it is an act done for oneself rather than the one who caused the pain. It is a personal healing process that cannot be transferred to the perpetrator.

The third misconception about forgiveness is that it is often not sustainable. Some think they can only forgive once or twice but certainly not seventy times seven, as the Bible says. People like to set conditions that should be met first to forgive. In the realm of marriage and family relationships, forgiveness should be ingrained as second nature. By "second nature," it doesn't imply thoughtless practice, as mindful forgiveness is essential for true healing. It should, however, stand as a non-negotiable core value within these relationships. Arthur and Kim Nowlin state: "We must learn to forgive and take the risk of establishing trust by nurturing and building a new trust through the spiritual relationship of our Christian walk."[29] This acknowledgment underscores that forgiveness is an endeavor to construct a bridge into the future, relying on the mutual trust that Christians should extend toward one another.

Stress

A lot has been said about stress, and life today seems littered with stressors—in the home, at work, at school, and on the highway. You name it, stress is all around. Stress is characterized as the burden of worry or unresolved issues that induce physical, mental, emotional, or spiritual tension, occasionally leading to illness, disease, or even

---

[29] Arthur & Kim Nowlin, *The Attitude Adjustment of the Christian Man and Woman* (Detroit, MI: Kim Logan Communications, 2004), p. 13.

death. Unaddressed stressors can contribute to irritability, impacting the dynamics of a marriage relationship. Notably, it has been observed that men and women often experience stress from distinct sources. For instance, men commonly experience stress stemming from job-related concerns, while women often find themselves stressed by matters related to the family. Drawing a parallel, another study on stressors revealed a similar pattern, indicating that men might be particularly affected by financial challenges, while women may find increased stress in relation to caregiving responsibilities. According to The Holmes and Rahe Stress Scale, the top ten most stressful life events showed the following results:[30]

➢ Death of a spouse (or child): 100

➢ Divorce: 73

➢ Marital separation: 65

➢ Imprisonment: 63

➢ Death of a close family member: 63

➢ Personal injury or illness: 53

➢ Marriage: 50

➢ Dismissal from work: 47

➢ Marital reconciliation: 45

➢ Retirement: 45

To fully understand the impact of stress, it is important to distinguish between static and dynamic stressors. Static stressors

---

[30] Paindoctor.com, *Top 10 Most Stressful Life Events: The Holmes and Rahe Stress Scale.* Accessed January 1, 2019.

are the kind you have no control over, such as the death of a family member, previous divorce, what happened in the past, or economic status. Sometimes, we worry about things we cannot control. Cherie Lowe, in *Focus on the Family*, uses the acronym FOMO (feeling of missing out). This is when the desire to want to enjoy what others are enjoying becomes a stressor. Dynamic stressors refer to those issues that individuals have the capacity to address and change. These may include miscommunication, abusive behaviors, negative attitudes, or a lack of commitment or motivation.

Robert M Sapolsky, in his book "Why Zebras Don't Get Ulcers," says that social support makes stressors less stressful. He emphasizes the need to get "social support from the right person, the right network of friends, the right community."[31] Proverbs 18:24 makes the same point: *"One who has unreliable friends soon comes to ruin, but there is a friend who sticks closer than a brother"* (NIV). An intimate relationship with the wrong person cannot reduce stress. For example, women who are in a bad marriage suffer from immune suppression.

Infidelity

In his documentary research titled "Predictably Irrational,"[32] Dan Ariely talks about cognitive dissonance—the lack of alignment between belief and behavior. He discovered that people who believed in the Ten Commandments often broke them when they were under pressure. He cited situations of people dating who knew that fornication was a sin but, when kissing each other, lacked the will power to resist the stimulus to commit a sexual act.

James Smith gives reasons why men and women cheat on each other. Men cheat on their wives for the following reasons:[33]

---

[31] Robert M. Sapolsky, *Why Zebras Don't Get Ulcers* (New York: Henry Holt Company, 2004), pp. 406-407.

[32] Dan Ariely, "Predictably Irrational: The Hidden Forces that Shape Our Decisions." CDs read by Simon Jones.

[33] James Smith, *Worried Lovers: Why do people cheat?* Worriedlovers.com. Accessed September 2018.

➢ Lack of intimacy

➢ Wife's failure to maintain her attractiveness

➢ Pretext to marry another woman who is already in the picture

➢ Addiction to sex (hypersexuality)

➢ Satisfying one's ego (being generally liked by women)

➢ Revenge—using another woman to get back at the petty wife

➢ Immaturity—short-sightedness and lack of self-control

Conversely, women may engage in infidelity for nearly identical reasons, with the exception that the second and third factors are supplanted by a lack of communication and independent behavior or a failure to engage in shared activities. Referring to the fourth aspect on the list, Genesis 4:1 challenges the notion of sex addiction by emphasizing Adam's profound knowledge of his wife, Eve. This biblical perspective underscores that sexual union, as designed by God, signifies oneness and a complete understanding of the other person on social, physical, emotional, and spiritual levels. Furthermore, it emphasizes that sex is a sacred and reserved act meant for the confines of marriage.

William M. Wilson, President of Oral Roberts University, talked about heavenly sex as inspired intimacy from God.[34] Accordingly, sex is protected (Ex 10:14; 1 Co 6:9-10), pleasurable (Pro 5:15-19), procreative (Gen. 1:28), passionate (Songs 1:2; 2:16), practiced regularly (1 Co 7:25), purified (He 13:4; Phil 2:4), and a prayerful act (Eccl 9:9; Gen 2:25).

In Song of Songs 2:8-17, love and sex are in tension. The lover visits his beloved and looks through the lattice while she is sleeping. He invites her to come out of the house so they can go out and be together in the beautiful spring. The language of sex is used without suggesting they are involved since they are not yet married. What is being suggested

---

[34] William M. Wilson on television channel TBN, October 5, 2013.

above is that sex consummates marriage and not marriage, sex. In other words, sex is to be only in the context of marriage. Another point one gets after reading Songs of Songs (3:1-5) is that the sexual passion that lovers have for each other exemplifies the passion we should have in our relationship with God, especially when going to church to worship. That sense of anticipation should be equally great.

If everything we do in life is an act of worship, sex, too, is an act of worship. God has a stake in it as well. Unfortunately, according to Myles Munroe, people are looking for sex without love, love without marriage, and marriage without responsibility.[35] In essence, individuals driven by the desire to please themselves may view sex as a performance rather than an experience. It's important to recognize that while sex can be an expression of love, it does not inherently create love. Love is a multifaceted and complex emotion that extends beyond physical intimacy. Joyce Meyer, in one of her speaking conferences, used the text in 1 Peter 3:11 that says we must make peace. Meyer told her audience: "Don't just make peace with others; first make peace with yourself." She went on to be more dynamic and graphic: "Make peace with your thing; make peace with your thighs." Wow!

Marriage Preparation

It's intriguing that the initial decision couples make is about the when and where of their marriage; yet the fundamental questions of why they want to get married and who their partner truly is may lack clarity. Frequently, their response to the first question revolves around "because we love each other," not realizing that love can be unpredictable and, at times, unsustainable. Pastor Shane Anderson, in his sermon titled *"How to Stay Married Forever & Like It,"* said couples must remember that they are not marrying only for *love* but for *life*.[36] The question about *who* they are marrying is tricky. They obviously

---

[35] Munroe, *Myles Munroe on Relationships* (Nassau, Bahamas: Bahamas Faith Ministries International, 2008), p. 235.
[36] Shane Anderson, "How to Stay Married Forever & Like It," sermon preached at Pioneer Memorial Church, Berrien Springs, Michigan, October 14, 2023.

know each other's names, but they don't know each other well. Anderson suggested that to know each other well, the couple must date each other for at least two years.

In general, couples often show more motivation to invest in the financial aspects of the wedding ceremony than in pre-marriage education or counseling. A significant portion of the wedding budget is allocated to meeting external expectations that may not necessarily align with the couple's personal needs and dynamics. However, it should be compelling to have the couple invest a little more financial resources toward pre-marriage education during their dating experience. Regrettably, numerous couples enter into marriage without sufficient preparation despite being well-prepared to financially support the wedding ceremony itself.

Also, what we have seen over the years is that some couples seek counseling as a requirement stipulated by the marriage officer. In a situation like that, the couple may not be emotionally committed to the counseling. They just want to get it over with. It's like a seminary student who studies Greek and Hebrew only to get a degree but forget everything after graduation. Marriage preparation alone is not enough. Couples require ongoing marriage enrichment to nurture and strengthen their relationship. This continuous effort involves activities that spouses engage in throughout their married life, not solely to address problems but to proactively prevent them. Based on our experience working with married couples, attending an enrichment seminar together is often more accessible for couples than seeking counseling to resolve a specific problem, which can sometimes feel as challenging as pulling teeth.

Parenting and Step-Parenting

While watching a program on television one day, someone said the home is the most dangerous place for a child today. The person was referring to the forms of abuse children go through at home. What an unforgettable truth if this is what a home has become! A home should be a little heaven on earth. It should be a safe place for every child. This means parents must be equipped with the skills needed to maintain a good relationship with each other and offer a conducive environment for the growth of the child. The plight of children today can no longer be ignored. These helpless "angels" are entirely dependent on parents and guardians for everything. Unresolved family conflicts, parental separation, divorce, and child abuse, for example, traumatize children severely. George Barna, a research guru, correctly states:

> As children mature, they are faced with numerous questions and choices regarding how to live. They take cues from their environment - particularly from the people they trust - as to how to respond to the dozens of choices they make every day. Unless children are shown the moral and spiritual implications of their choices, such factors are overloaded, often resulting in unfortunate or unforeseen consequences.[37]

Family Dynamics

It is a fact that the African traditional family is changing due to economic constraints, globalization, and pluralization. The conventional structure of the two-parent married nuclear family, supporting biological offspring, is undergoing a transformation as alternative family forms become more prevalent. This shift includes the emergence of single-parent families, unwed mothers and fathers, same-sex couples, a growing demand for adoptions, the rise of stay-at-home dads, blended families with stepsiblings, interracial marriages, homeless families, and couples choosing to remain childfree by choice.[38] The role of the extended family of aunts, uncles, grandparents, and cousins is becoming less prevalent as a player in a couple's marriage and

---

[37] George Barna, *Transforming Children into Spiritual Champions* (Venture, CA: Regal Books, 2003), p. 30.
[38] For more discussion, see Andrew J. Weaver, Linda A. Revila & Harold G. Koenig, *Counseling Families Across the Stages of Life* (Nashville, TN: Abingdon Press, 2002).

relationship. Roles and relationships are being redefined by referring to them as married partners and unwed partners.

Sickness and Death

Sickness and death are often overlooked in discussions about marriage and family issues, yet these are profound experiences that can swiftly alter the dynamics of a family. These challenges have the potential to bring significant changes and emotional upheavals, underscoring the importance of addressing them within the broader conversation about family dynamics. Traditionally, Africans didn't have health or life insurance policies. In cases of emergency, their security lay in the number of cattle one had and the free communal support system. In the present day, a considerable number of Africans residing abroad have secured health and life insurance yet lack the traditional support system inherent in their home countries. Consequently, when faced with sickness or death, they find themselves vulnerable. While many Africans in the diaspora may possess health policies or partial access to healthcare coverage, a notable gap exists in the availability of comprehensive life policies that adequately cover death-related expenses and funeral arrangements.

Traditionally, Africans don't talk about death and funeral planning in advance. As a result, if a member of the family dies, there's reliance on fundraising events or online giving programs to raise funds for the funerals. In some cases, this involves transporting the remains back to Africa. The communal spirit of Africans abroad is enviable, especially when tragedy strikes. However, the communal benevolence of Africans is often overtaxed due to the unusual frequency of deaths that occur. Such benevolence has not come without other challenges. Regrettably, the proliferation of appeals has prompted some individuals to contribute based on factors such as the status, prestige, region, tribe, or ethnicity of the deceased. Even within diverse and cross-cultural African communities in the diaspora, this divisive spirit has surfaced, leading to the fragmentation of these communities.

While this spirit of unity and communalism is to be encouraged, it is hoped that every African family in the diaspora will look seriously at life policies to alleviate the stress and the imbalanced giving. Besides, such policies will ensure that the surviving members are cared for.

There was a period when our children were young and reliant on us for everything. As parents, we grappled with the concern of the unforeseen circumstance of being involved in an accident, leaving behind children without a guardian. The thought of returning them to Africa, a place they hadn't known intimately due to a life spent in the diaspora, added an extra layer of potential trauma.

Adjusting to the situation back in Africa would be quite challenging for them. Many families can attest to this. Hence, the need for each family to plan as much as possible so that surviving members can be given a sense of security.

APPLICATION: After reading this chapter, which challenges do you face that affect your marriage or family relationships?

CHAPTER 3

ROOTS OF MARRIAGE PROBLEMS AMONG AFRICANS IN THE DIASPORA

"If you are teachable, you are fixable." Ron Rockey

The challenges in marriage and family discussed in chapter two are symptoms of salient causes that need attention. Often, people hastily attempt to resolve the symptoms without delving into the root causes. Willard F. Harley (2002) outlined six love busters that can undermine marital relationships. These include selfish demands, disrespectful judgments, angry outbursts, dishonesty, annoying habits, and independent behavior. Addressing these fundamental issues is crucial for fostering a healthy and enduring marriage.[39] These six attitudes and behaviors apply to marriage relationships across cultures. In addition to these, there are other reasons why African marriages in the diaspora are impacted negatively. Our purpose is to identify, discuss, and suggest how these underlying causes can be reversed with the hope of strengthening African marriages and families in the diaspora.

---

[39] Willard F. Harley Jr, *Love Busters: Overcoming Habits That Destroy Romantic Love* (Grand Rapids, MI: Fleming H. Revell, 2002).

Lack of Information and Strategies for Healthy Family Relationships

As stated before, many couples enter a marriage relationship quite unprepared, mentally, psychologically, and spiritually. Even though they are highly emotionally connected, they lack an in-depth pre-marital education or counseling that covers a wide range of issues. As observed earlier, counseling is taken as a mere prerequisite or just a step that is needed to confirm the wedding date that is already fixed. Instead, pre-marital education should inform rather than confirm. Sufficient time should be dedicated to counseling practices. Unfortunately, due to demanding schedules, pastors often find themselves unable to conduct extensive counseling sessions.

Whether pre-marital education is done by a certified counselor or a pastor, it is important that it be done well in advance, even before the wedding date is set. Counseling must be a pre-requisite for setting the wedding date and not the other way around. This gives the couple time to internalize, visualize, and then commit themselves to the marriage relationship. They need to enter marriage having understood what it takes to grow a happy, healthy, and holy family.

Howard. H. Mattison, a theology teacher at Solusi University, used to say, "I eat not because I am hungry but to prevent hunger." There may be some truth to that. Not only is prevention better than cure, but it is also cheaper. Dr. Jerry M. Lewis, Chief Psychiatrist in Dallas, Texas, said, "It is the quality of the couple's relationship that sets the stage for giving birth to a healthy family."[40] When couples and families pursue a preventive and pro-solution attitude, relationships will be happy, healthy, and holy. It should not be assumed that pre-marriage counseling is all that the couple needs. There's a need for post-wedding growth seminars for couples to avail themselves of. Reiterating, couples should not wait until problems arise before engaging in marriage enrichment seminars. Unfortunately, many couples invest more time

---

[40] Quoted in G. Curtis Jones, *1000 Illustrations for Preaching and Teaching* (Nashville, TN: Broadman & Holman Publishers, 1996), p. 134.

and effort in preparing for their wedding day than they do for the entirety of their marriage.

It is often said that those who work in the reserve bank are trained to recognize counterfeit paper money by teaching them what genuine money looks like and feels like. This should be the same approach as pre-marital counseling. Pre-marital counseling is often viewed in terms of dos and don'ts, focusing on potential problems in marriage rather than emphasizing the blessings it brings. It is essential for counseling to accentuate the positive aspects of marriage, providing a vision of what a loving marital relationship entails. The Song of Solomon, for example, offers a positive approach to intimate relationships and can serve as a grounding and inspirational foundation for couples. Highlighting the blessings and promises bestowed by God upon those entering marriage is crucial, and from a Christian perspective, incorporating the Bible plays a key role in counseling. This will be covered in chapter four when we deal with Biblical thinking. Ellen G. White had this to say to couples:[41]

> My Dear Brother and Sister: You have united in a lifelong covenant. Your education in married life has begun. The first year of married life is a year of experience, a year in which husband and wife learn each other's different traits of character, as a child learns lessons in school. In this, the first year of your married life, let there be no chapters that will mar your future happiness.... – {The Adventist Home, p.102.5}

> My brother, your wife's time and, strength, and happiness are now bound up with yours. Your influence over her may be a savor of life unto life or of death unto death. Be very careful not to spoil her life. – {The Adventist Home, p. 103.1}

---

[41] Ellen G. White, *The Adventist Home* (Hagerstown, MD: Review and Herald Publishing Association, 1952), pp. 102-103.

My sister, you are now to learn your first practical lessons regarding the responsibilities of married life. Be sure to learn these lessons faithfully day by day.... Guard constantly against giving way to selfishness. – {The Adventist Home, p. 103.2}

In your life union, your affections are to be tributary to each other's happiness. Each is to minister to the happiness of the other. This is the will of God concerning you. But while you are to blend as one, neither of you is to lose his or her individuality in the other. God is the owner of your individuality. Of Him, you are to ask: What is right? What is wrong? How may I best fulfill the purpose of my creation? – {The Adventist Home, p. 103.3}

God has ordained that there should be perfect love and harmony between those who enter the marriage relation. Let bride and bridegroom, in the presence of the heavenly universe, pledge themselves to love each other as God has ordained, they should.... The wife is to respect and reverence her husband, and the husband is to love and cherish his wife. -- {The Adventist Home, p. 103.4}

These are some of the lessons to be mastered before a marriage relationship begins.

Unwillingness to Adjust and Modify Traditional Family Roles

Traditional gender roles contribute to tensions in marriages. Jean Davison highlights two perspectives on women's roles, one of which is articulated by Rudo Gaidzanwa (1992:109). Gaidzanwa expresses concern about the oppressive nature of patrilineal cultures in Africa, particularly in their treatment of exceptional women. In Gaidzanwa's view, patrilineal cultures make it impossible for women to lead or achieve autonomy.[42] The contrasting view is that advanced by Kamene Okonjo of Nigeria, who observes what she calls a "dual-sex political system" among the Igbos of Nigeria. This means, according to Okonjo, women and men of high rank had comparable and complementary positions.[43] In the case of Gaidzanwa, it should be noted that she speaks from the platform of the feminist movement that seeks to achieve gender equality.

Along the same line, Moreblessing Tandeka Tinarwo and Dominic Pasura published a study about "transnational and global" migrations of Zimbabweans. In this study, they assert that the mobility and migration of Zimbabwe's women have increased opportunities for them in their quest for freedom, power, and decision-making, particularly within their households.[44] They also observe that the numbers of migrant women have outnumbered that of men in South Africa, the United Kingdom, Australia, and elsewhere. Whereas in the colonial era, men were breadwinners and women were housekeepers and childminders, this forced women into dependence on men, and eroded their access to resources and opportunities.[45]

Tinarwo and Pasura continue to suggest that the traditional and cultural structures in post-independent Zimbabwe have been restrictive of women in making decisions such as owning property unless they do so under the umbrella of marriage. They also observe that the institution of marriage is still significant in the configuration of power, space, and identity for women.[46]

The quest for meaning among women has discovered its resolution in job opportunities in the diaspora. It is reasonable to suggest that the

---

[42] Jean Davison, *Gender, Lineage, and Ethnicity in Southern Africa* (Boulder, CO: Westview Press, 1997), p. 35

[43] Ibid., p. 37.

[44] Moreblessing Tandeka Tinarwo and Dominic Pasura, "Negotiating and Contesting Gendered and Sexual Identities in the Zimbabwean Diaspora" (Journal of Southern African Studies, Vol. 40, No. 3, 2014), p. 524.

[45] Ibid., p. 523.

[46] Ibid., p. 523.

experience of Zimbabwean women mirrors that of women across Africa. The intersection between traditional norms and the evolving roles of women in the diaspora, when not navigated carefully, introduces stress into marriage and family relationships. Many married women have ventured abroad in pursuit of job opportunities, leaving their husbands and children behind or having them follow later as dependents. Upon reunification, gender roles, which were not a source of conflict while in Africa, can become subjects of disdain and contempt.[47]

The shame this creates, particularly among men, makes it difficult to assume traditional roles, especially when both spouses are professionals who work outside the home. Africans living in the United States, for example, find themselves going with the flow to realize the so-called American Dream. What was generally known to be the "land that flowed with milk and honey" is no longer the case. What Africans have come to discover is that to enjoy the milk and the honey, they must breed their own cows and bees, respectively. Thus, they work around the clock doing more than one job and going through school at the same time.

Faced with these dilemmas and financial demands, both parents, along with any eligible children, often find it necessary to work to meet their financial obligations. This places pressure on the family to make adjustments in various roles, including cooking, house cleaning, changing baby diapers, doing laundry, driving, shopping, and even changing tires on the car. Flexibility in sharing these responsibilities becomes essential. Any resistance to adapt can have repercussions not only on the couple's relationship but also on their relationships with the broader family.

In the Zulu tradition, one of the husband's expected duties toward his wife is to act as guardian, legally and socially. A married woman is always a minor, requiring her husband to act on her behalf.[48] Coming from a Ndebele tradition that shared the same view, I (Zebron) had a

---

[47] For more discussion on gender roles, see Carolyn Schrock-Shenk, ed. *Mediation and Facilitation Training Manual* (Akron, PA: Mennonite Conciliation Service, 2000), p. 113.

[48] D. H. Reader, *Zulu Tribe in Transition* (Manchester: Manchester University Press, 1966), p. 160.

rude awakening some years ago when Peggie and I were at Andrews University in the United States. One day, I went to see Dr. Elaine Giddings, then chair of the communication department, to talk about Peggie's desire to register as a student. It came as a bombshell to me when Dr. Giddings asked me: "Where is Peggie? I want her to speak for herself." What a rude awakening! That was a game-changer for me going forward. This is one example where traditional norms, if not modified, can affect relationships in the diaspora. Unfortunately, this has not been easy for African families to do. As a result, it has caused a divide between couples, resulting in separation and divorce. Due to these challenges, homicides and domestic violence are on the increase as well.

Collision Between Cultural and Market Norms

Social norms are community-based, fostering a collective spirit where individuals engage in communal activities or assist each other without expecting monetary compensation. Extended family members and neighbors often come forward to offer support and relieve the family before pressures reach a critical point. For example, when a mother needs assistance with babysitting, a neighbor or relative will volunteer to help. There's no talk about payment. It is generally understood that in the future, there will be a return of favor. It is important to note that doing so is considered being "human" or *ubuntu*, the African philosophy of life. Oliver A. Onwubiko cites a Hausa proverb to show how human relations operate in Africa: *"Friendship with the ferryman right from the dry season means that when the rains come, you will be the first to cross."*[49] This proverb explains how social norms work in African cultural contexts. Failure to reciprocate a good gesture is seen as being antisocial.

In contrast, market norms thrive on direct and immediate exchanges of goods and services. For example, if you require a babysitter, you may either hire one or take your child to a daycare center. Courtesies in such contexts are often reciprocated in financial terms, aligning with

---

[49] Oliver A. Onwubiko, p. 19. Emphasis not supplied.

the principle that time is money and everything comes with a cost. This thinking is rooted in individualism, reflecting the notion of "every man for himself." As a result, a collision between social and market norms often results in the weakening of traditional social norms. When these courtesies are no longer available in the community, problems in marriage begin to show up.

Ubuntu philosophy is embedded in African family relationships so that when social and market norms collide at the workplace, one is forced to make a choice between work and family expectations. In the context of a work environment, when a member of one's family gets ill or dies, *ubuntu* philosophy dictates that one must travel and attend to the crisis. This frequently entails taking time away from work and traveling to Africa for an extended period to attend to illness or death in the family. However, this can create a conflict with one's employer, as market norms within the workplace often prioritize profitability in business. The clash of these norms places individuals in the difficult position of having to choose between job commitments and family relations.

There's also the pressure to balance the scales of practicing *ubuntu* towards one's own family and the spouse's family. Failure to strike a balance between work commitments and family obligations can lead to conflicts in marital relationships. Consequently, many couples feel compelled to spend money and resources on trips, often accumulating debt, which adds an additional stressor to their marriage. Consequently, couples may find themselves caught in the whirlwind of meeting the needs of their extended family.

To resolve this dilemma, the couple needs to unify its goals and rank its priorities to avoid competition. To achieve this, there must be a conversation where the couple listens and opens so that no one is left guessing what the other thinks and how he/she feels. When this happens, anything the couple agrees on will stand and will be a factor in the decision-making process, especially when challenges emerge. The couple should avoid doing anything without the enthusiastic support of the other, especially in areas that have a potential for conflict. The couple should realize that not all cultural expectations or commitments can be met. In this case, a simple expression of genuine apology can resolve the dilemma if it is done equally to both families.

Lack of Skills to Preserve Values and Adapt Methods

It is pertinent to begin by clarifying the concept of African values. African traditions are incredibly diverse, making it impossible to confine them to a singular location or situation. Nevertheless, a unifying cultural thread among Africans is the philosophy of ubuntu. This word, as discussed before, expresses what it means to be human in the context of community. The word *ubuntu* carries a set of cultural values that are shared across Africa, and here we just highlight a few:

> ➤ Being communal (finding and experiencing one's identity and meaning within the community).

> ➤ Being hospitable (showing kindness to extended family, strangers, and passersby).

> ➤ Being social (doing things that unite people; shunning that which is evil—witchcraft, gossip).

> ➤ Being religious (practicing religion in all aspects of life; participating in sacred rituals and festivals).

> ➤ Being respectful (respecting elders, community leaders, and sacred authorities).

> ➤ Being a master of time (doing many things at the same time). On this matter, Oliver Onwubiko says that Africans don't keep clock time because they are masters of time. Their view of time is socialized time.[50] An African woman can multi-task by cooking, grinding, and attending to her baby all at the same time. An African is never late because he/she is a master of time.

---

[50] Onwubiko, pp. 25, 27.

He/she must attend to more than one thing. What is important is arriving and not punctuality because other pressing things were considered equally important. It is not uncommon for Africans to attend three events on the same day because they understand that failure to show up on any is lack of *ubuntu*.

> Being communicative (learning the language, idioms, and myths that express thought patterns and explain culture). It is believed that one cannot understand people unless he/she learns their language. This brings us to the discussion below about raising children in the diaspora.

Africans in the diaspora grapple with the challenge of preserving their aforementioned values while simultaneously adapting to their host culture. Responses to this predicament vary widely. Some individuals have successfully found alternative coping mechanisms that do not compromise their cultural and religious values. Others have adopted a strategy of denial, adhering strictly to traditional ways until the situation becomes unmanageable. There are also those who choose to compromise their African values and, at times, even Christian values in order to align with local expectations and demands.

The area that has experienced the most challenges is the raising of children in a host culture. It drives some parents nuts when their children cannot speak their vernacular language or behave in African ways. Yet there are other parents who seem to take pride that their children no longer speak or understand their own language. Parents often find themselves in a state of confusion, unsure of the best course of action. Striking a balance requires parents to possess the skills to identify non-negotiable aspects while also being willing to let go of certain cultural elements in favor of embracing the host culture. As noted by George Allan Phiri, when navigating the complexities of culture and customs, specific considerations should be considered:[51]

---

[51] George Allan Phiri, *Socio-Cultural Anthropology: Christian Communication and the African Culture* (Eugene, Oregon: Resource Publications, 2009), pp. 73-74.

➢ That African cultures, like all other cultures, are a product of depraved and evil minds (Rom. 1:18-32). They cannot be safely and solely relied upon.

➢ That God is the absolute reality of humankind if cultural change will occur.

➢ That culture can be deceptive because those who practice it are subjective; they interpret reality from their worldview.

➢ That culture is ethnocentric and generational; the gospel is universal and transgenerational.

➢ That people who practice culture have wrong concepts about the gospel and Christ; that is, they are more likely to misinterpret and distort the gospel.

In view of the above considerations, we recommend that couples should take the following steps to sort out what should be discarded and what should be embraced in culture:

➢ Draw lines on matters of cultural preferences; such should not be used as a principle for everybody.

➢ Reject cultural practices that are explicitly prohibited by Scripture—the basis for absolutes.

➢ Replace such practices with the Lordship of Christ. This means upholding the supremacy and sufficiency of Jesus Christ. He is the Way, the Truth, and the Life; He is the Bread and the Water of life (Jn. 14:6; 6:35).

➢ Distinguish several categories of customs:

  • Those to be renounced immediately because they are condemned by Scripture.

- Patience on behavior and thinking that will disappear as reality changes.

- Customs (not morals) labeled as being indifferent and are to be left to one's discretion.

➤ Consider the problem of association—when a harmless practice in one culture is associated with that which is evil in another culture. A practice may be harmless and offensive at the same time when associated with another evil practice. Willian Hendriksen put it well: "In things essential unity. In doubtful things liberty. In all things charity."[52]

Children, too, grapple with their own frustrations in this dynamic. They seek to assimilate with their peers in the host culture while simultaneously being tasked with upholding family expectations. This inherent tension often gives rise to third-culture children, who find themselves in a space where they neither completely fit into the host culture nor fully identify with their familial expectations. This cultural dissonance can prove to traumatize both parents and children, disrupting the essential fabric or system the family requires to thrive.

Third-culture children are also cross-cultural children (kids)— "those who have interacted or are interacting significantly with two or more cultural worlds during their childhood."[53] These children are caught between their first (home or passport) culture and the second (host or local) culture. This puts them in a neither/nor world of existence called *third culture*.[54] Those born and growing up in a host culture find themselves at odds with their parents' home cultural values as well as their own identity within a host culture that views them as belonging to a minority subculture.

Parents require guidance on maintaining effective communication

---

[52] William Hendriksen, New Testament Commentary, Luke. Grand Rapids: Baker, p. 632.
[53] Pollock, Van Reken, and Pollock, p. xv.
[54] Ibid., p. 17.

with their children without becoming obsolete. This involves actively listening to and paying attention to their children's concerns without passing judgment or labeling them as deviant. Rather than attacking behavior, it's crucial to teach values. Fostering an atmosphere of openness encourages children to share even the most challenging concerns, including aspects traditionally deemed taboo, such as dating and sexual drives. Further insights on parenting and step-parenting will be elaborated in Chapter 9.

Prioritizing Roles Above Relationship Building

Over time, individuals in a relationship may find themselves taking each other for granted. For many couples, after the initial excitement of marriage fades, intimacy can gradually take a back seat. The emphasis shifts from simply being together to getting caught up in numerous activities. Couples may unintentionally adopt a lifestyle akin to that of married singles, where they focus more on fulfilling cultural roles through various tasks, losing intimacy in the process. This tendency often surfaces during the middle years of marriage when children become the central focus. Both partners may find themselves prioritizing the needs of their children over each other's, inadvertently diminishing the intimacy in their relationship.

To survive, love between husband and wife needs three ingredients: *passion*, *intimacy*, and *commitment*.[55] What often happens is that instead of making sure that all three aspects of the love triangle are fulfilled, the couple may just be coasting along, assuming that fulfilling roles is all that is needed.

Passion, by its very nature, is sacrificial, meaning you are motivated to suffer for something. Jessica Bethoney says passion can be very difficult to slow down because, once ignited, it "requires obstacles to

---

[55] David Olsen, John DeFrain, and Linda Skogrand, pp. 249-250. See also a comment in Life Application Bible Study on Malachi 2:15-16, p. 1971: "We need passion in the marriage relationship to keep the commitment and intimacy satisfying but this passion should be focused exclusively on our spouse."

fan its flames."[56] It is expressed through touching, kissing, and being affectionate. As such, it can develop quickly and fade quickly. It can make you feel that you are "in love" with a person you neither really know nor necessarily like.

According to Bethoney, such a heightened state of passionate love cannot be sustained in marriage.[57] This is why it should not be the couple's only focus on the relationship. *Intimacy* is an emotional experience that involves sharing feelings, providing emotional support, and feeling safe with high levels of self-disclosure, including the sharing of personal information. This means there should be conversation and active listening between husband and wife. *Commitment* is cerebral, which means it is a mental connection with and an attachment to another person. The couple does this by moving the relationship to the next level, for example, from dating to engagement and then to marriage. It is what the couple means when they say, "In sickness and in health, in prosperity or adversity; and forsaking all others, I will keep myself only to you, so long as we both shall live."

This love triangle requires staying faithful in the relationship, even during difficult times. When the couple experiences only one aspect of the love triangle more than the other two, the relationship will not be healthy. For example:

➢ Passion without intimacy and commitment reduces the relationship to *gratification.*

➢ Intimacy without passion and commitment reduces the relationship to *attraction.*

➢ Commitment without intimacy and passion reduces the relationship to *tradition.*

Also, the couple may short-change themselves when they experience

---

[56] Jessica Bethoney, "The Myth of Passion," in Janice R. Levine and Howard J. Markman, eds. *Why do fools fall in love?* (San Francisco, CA: Jossey-Bass, 2001), p. 16.
[57] Ibid., p. 17.

two aspects of the love triangle and starve each other of the third. For example:

➢ Intimacy and passion without commitment mean the relationship has no *accountability*.

➢ Commitment and passion without intimacy mean the relationship has no *communication*.

➢ Intimacy and commitment without passion mean the relationship has no *fire*.

Relationship building means couples must have all three dimensions (commitment, intimacy, and passion) in their relationship. The three flesh out what love means. However, love, by its very nature, is puzzling; all it does is help get the relationship off to a good start, but it is not sufficient in making the relationship last. The couple needs to have relationship skills.[58] For example, after the honeymoon, the couple must get back to work. Imagine the husband telling his wife, "I'm not going to work today because I love you so much and want to spend time with you all day." This is what Patricia Love means when she says that within two years, a marriage relationship undergoes a natural state of neutrality. "At this point, you must rely upon your relational skills to keep love alive."[59] And Jessica Bethoney adds, "True marriage can begin only when passion [honeymoon] wanes."[60]

In today's individualistic society, there exists a yearning for intimacy among married couples that passion alone cannot fully satisfy. Intimacy encompasses a quadrant comprising emotional, physical, social, and spiritual needs and expressions of spouses. It is imperative to address all four aspects of this quadrant to maintain a sustainable marital relationship. However, it is common for spouses to

---

[58] Amy and David Olsen, "Traits of Love," in *Why do fools fall in love?* Edited by Janice R. Levine and Howard J. Markman, pp. 185-189.

[59] Patricia Love, "Fool's Love," *Why do fools fall in love?* p. 13.

[60] Jessica Bethoney, "The Myth of Passion," in *Why do fools fall in love?* p. 18.

focus on one or two elements at the expense of the others. This selective attention is akin to knowingly attempting to drive a car with a flat tire—an endeavor that risks not only damaging the tire but potentially harming other parts of the car, leading to a possible accident.

The intimacy quadrant below shows the wholistic (holistic) nature of being human—emotional, physical, social, and spiritual. When any one of these facets is ignored, a human being is not complete.

EMOTIONAL	PHYSICAL
Sharing goals, insights, beliefs, and interests	Touching, talking, looking, smelling, and conjugal rights.
SOCIAL	SPIRITUAL
Being involved in activities and hobbies together	Spending time together in worship, prayer, study, and devotion

Diagram 1. Intimacy Quadrants

Each quadrant represents an ongoing task for spouses, demanding continual maintenance and effort to cultivate intimacy and ensure the longevity of the relationship. The middle years of marriage are particularly vulnerable due to the demands of work and parenting. The desire to fulfill culturally defined roles during this phase can inadvertently overshadow the nurturing of intimacy, making it essential for couples to be mindful and deliberate in sustaining all facets of the relationship. Sometimes familiarity and inertia cause spouses to take each other for granted and thus relax while doing their homework.

Leaving the Home Front Unguarded

Thanks for the sacrifice of men and women in the military who keep the rest of us safe. They sometimes have to fight battles far away from home, being separated from their spouses and children who are left behind. Even though the nation's home front is technologically protected and guarded, the families themselves endure a lot of distress caused by the long absence of a military family member. The anxiety levels are high on both ends. Sadly, there are instances when infidelity is irresistible and regrettable.

The Bible in 1 Samuel 30 talks about the experience of David, a well trained military man, who raided the Amelekites in a hill country, away from home. While this happened, the Amelekites attacked David's home front in Ziglag, burned it down, and carried away the people, including his wives. Upon discovering this tragedy, David sought counsel from Abiathar the priest, and with 600 soldiers he pursued the Amelekites. He defeated the enemy and recovered everything that had been taken, including his wives.

The above instances are instructive of what sometimes happens among African families in the diaspora. As immigrants, Africans often have to undertake activities that keep them very busy trying to make ends meet. They have busy work schedules and educational commitments in order to maintain their visa stutus. Meanwhile, the home front is left unguarded and vulnerable to invading negative influences, such as feelings of anxiety, loneliness, rejection, abandonment, and boredom. These feelings become the gateway to the use of ellicit drugs and alcoholic addiction.

The busy schedules have negative impact not only on children but also on parents themselves, since they lack quality time together. One would expect that weekends and public holidays offer an opportunity for the families to enjoy time together; but these are sometimes occasions when they pick up overtime in order to make ends meet.

The demand to be busy also comes from the pressure to support family members back home in Africa. The African philosophy of Ubuntu is irresistible. It teaches one to be social, respectful, accountable, and communal. Thus, extended family relationships have to be constantly maintained because failure to do so cuts one off the needed lifeline. This sometimes adds pressure on the diaspora families to overstretch and overextend themselves socially and economically. The vicious cycle of meeting the expectations back home and balancing the demands of the home front is endless. To avoid this cycle, individuals need to set some boundaries, to be discussed later in this book.

Lack of Sexual Fulfillment

Related to the discussion about prioritizing role over relationship building is the problem of lack of sexual fulfillment in African marriages in the diaspora. Sexual dissatisfaction is a widespread concern transcending cultural and geographical boundaries. However, this discussion centers on Africans in the diaspora due to the demanding nature of their schedules. As previously highlighted, individuals in the diaspora often extend themselves across home, school, and workplace responsibilities to make ends meet. Unfortunately, in this juggling act, the home front frequently ends up receiving less attention and prioritization.

The one area that gets the raw end of the deal is sexual intimacy. In most cases, husband and wife are not home at the same time due to the rhythm of their schedules. That means they don't have normal conjugal access to each other. Intimacy is compromised. Even when they are both at home at the same time, they experience low energy due to overwork. This impacts their conjugal activity negatively.

A common observation is that husbands often lament that wives find every excuse to avoid sexual relations. Conversely, wives frequently complain that husbands expect to reap benefits without putting in the effort of tilling, cultivating, and nurturing the emotional connection. In essence, they desire sex without love—an absence of emotional bonding. Consequently, both partners find themselves lacking sexual fulfillment, leading to feelings of irritability, agitation, and edginess over trivial matters. This discontent opens the door to disharmony and disunity in the relationship.

Quite often, the onus is on the man to find a way to rejuvenate intimacy in the relationship. Cassalnnie Henry states: "At the outset of a relationship, the man, in most cases, does not perceive the needs of the woman. Instead, he is more concerned about his needs and the satisfaction of his desires."[61] Henry goes on to identify basic needs of a woman that must be met by a man in marriage. She needs to be loved by showing unconditional love. In Greek, it is *agape*, sacrificial love. She wants to feel secure. In a relationship, a woman often seeks three crucial assurances from her partner. The man must demonstrate that the relationship is permanent, stable, and enduring. He is expected to protect and provide for her and the family. Lastly, she desires assurance that he genuinely loves her, conveyed through both actions and words. Henry points out, "Fear of losing her man drives her to seek solutions from other sources." This underlying fear can become the foundation for infidelity if these assurances are not fulfilled.

Conjugal performance is critical to sustaining emotional intimacy in marriage. Women often say that after the physical act, they are left to feel they have been used. This is when the man quickly falls asleep after an act that did not reach the desired mutual climax. To avert this, Henry suggests five stages for intimate and fulfilling sexual act:[62] (1) *Preplay* (preparation and priming for conjugal activity by touching, hugging, and expressions of appreciation), (2) *Foreplay* (stimulating the sensitivity of appropriate anatomical area leading to the act), (3) *Engagement* (positioning and awareness of partner's needs), (4) *Postplay* (attitude exhibited after the act), and (5) *Replay* (repeat of *preplay* and making appropriate adjustments for better performance).

Mention must be made that communication between husband and wife is very critical during and after the activity. The wife should not make her husband feel inadequate sexually. Blame game is the surest way to kill both intimacy and relationship. Also, the husband should

---

[61] Casalnnie Henry, *Neutralizing the Power of Fear* (Bloomington, IN: iUniverse, 2008), p. 62.

[62] Ibid., pp. 70–72.

not require his wife to perform perverse or abnormal sexual acts. Using Romans 1:26, 27, where the Apostle Paul talks about changing the natural use for what is against nature, Casalnnie Henry writes:

> "A man should never ask or require his wife to perform sexual acts that are deviant acts. I will attempt to discreetly say that God gave mankind the gift of speaking, singing, and eating with his mouth and the ability to excrete with the organ designated for that purpose. We should glorify God with our whole being according to how he has made us."[63]

Dwelling on the Past Than on the Future

Certain couples invest a significant amount of their time and energy dwelling on the past rather than focusing on the future. Their disagreements often revolve around dredging up past events to support their arguments or make a point. When every discussion is anchored in the past, progress becomes stunted. The past, being static, offers limited opportunities for change, except perhaps as a source of learning. It's crucial for couples to shift their focus towards the future to foster growth and development in their relationship.

The more the couple focuses on the future, the better the relationship will be. We should take a cue from drivers. Every car has a windshield, a rearview mirror, and two side view mirrors. All are important, but the windshield is the most important one; this is why it is wider. It is meant to allow for a wider view of where you are going and to make sure that you spend more time looking ahead and seeing what is going on. Yes, from time to time, you need to watch what happens behind you and on the sides; this is why those mirrors are smaller in comparison.

Navigating marital conflicts is akin to using rear and side mirrors when driving. Learning from past mistakes is crucial for changing lanes in life, just as checking these mirrors is essential for changing

---

[63] Ibid., p. 71.

lanes on the road. Side mirrors enable us to become aware of peripheral issues in conflicts, preventing us from getting sidetracked by unrelated matters. While every relationship may encounter historical and side issues, dwelling excessively on them depletes the energy needed to strengthen the relationship. Thus, maintaining a forward-looking vision is imperative for the well-being of the marriage and family.

Failure to Recognize Male-Female Differences

Acknowledging the topic of male-female or gender differences often sparks controversial and divergent viewpoints, venturing into a complex and politically charged landscape. The debate surrounding whether these differences stem from biological factors or societal expectations is ongoing. In the context of marriage between a man and a woman, our objective is to delve into these differences and emphasize that failure to recognize and understand gender distinctions can lead to detrimental consequences in the marital relationship.

Gender identity develops early in infancy when gender is identified physiologically. Parents select a name for a child based on the child's gender; however, some names may be gender neutral. In this case, parents, families, peers, and teachers relate to the child according to the child's gender identification. *Gender roles* are the behaviors and characteristics that a culture teaches to males and females based on their biological sex. Feminine behaviors are expected of females and masculine of males.

Contemporary perspectives on gender roles emphasize a graded continuum, acknowledging that individuals exhibit varying degrees of masculinity and femininity, highlighting both differences and complementarity. Both men and women can embody aspects of both masculinity and femininity, a concept known as androgyny, particularly in various role-playing scenarios. It is increasingly common to witness men taking on tasks traditionally associated with femininity, such as changing baby diapers, and women engaging in activities typically linked to masculinity, like changing a flat tire on a car. Numerous studies confirm the existence of physiological and psychological differences between males and females. Importantly, these differences should not be exploited to perpetuate stereotypes or foster notions of superiority and inferiority. Willard F. Harley Jr. (online tutorial, 2013) says that male-female brains are different. He states:

> "They [brains of males and females] not only looked different, they functioned differently. I wanted each student to fully understand why men and women think differently. It's because their brains are different. Women have far more connections between the left and right hemispheres. The connecting band of fibers called the corpus callosum is much thicker in women than in men. There are more connections between neurons as well, and there are more neurons -- 12 billion more. And yet, their brain is smaller . . . There is a far greater difference between the brains of the average man and woman than there is between the brains of representative people of all racial groupings on earth. Racially and ethnically, we are essentially identical. Sexually, we are vastly different.
>
> But while I demonstrated the differences between the brains of men and women to my students, I stressed their equal value. They complement each other. The strengths and weaknesses of male cognition balance the strengths and weaknesses of female cognition. Together, they offer a more complete perspective on life than either can have on their own. All that's required for those specialized advantages to express themselves in real life is for every husband and wife to have profound respect for the differences in the way they viewed the world and think together to find mutually appealing solutions to the problems they face."

Benjamin B. Lahey observes male and female differences in cognitive ability and achievement.[64] On average, women score higher on tests in language skills, reading comprehension, spelling, verbal and spatial memory, perception skills, and fine motor skills. Men score higher than women on mechanical reasoning, mathematics, science and social studies achievements, computer science, electronics, and automotive skills. There's also evidence of differences in emotional and social behavior. Women are more likely to be nurturing and sympathetic, sociable and friendly, trusting and open, cooperative and conciliatory, anxious and depressed, and better able to hide emotions than men. On the other hand, men are more likely to be competitive and dominant, assertive, unafraid of risks, aggressive, and commit sex crimes. Males and females differ also in mating and sexual behavior. On one side, women are more likely to prefer an older mate, a mate who has a high earning potential, and a partner of good character. They are threatened more by emotional infidelity and restrict sex to potential long-term commitment. Men on the other side, prefer a young mate, a mate who is physically attractive, and a mate with good housekeeping skills. They are threatened by sexual infidelity, feel comfortable with the idea of casual sex for themselves, and are sexually jealous and controlling of their spouse.

Rick Johnson says males mature emotionally slower than females.[65] Girls develop the right side of the brain faster than boys, so they learn talking, vocabulary, reading, and memory better than boys. Boys develop the left side of the brain faster than girls, so they develop visual, logical, and problem-solving skills faster than girls. Johnson further observes that women have superior verbal skills than men. If they want to interact effectively with their men, women must learn to speak the men's language. Because they are not very proficient at verbal communication, men are suspicious or fearful of communication. Instead, men communicate through body language;

---

[64] Benjamin B. Lahey, *Psychology: An Introduction*, 9th ed. (New York: McGraw-Hill, 2007), pp. 409-411.
[65] Rick Johnson, *How to talk so your husband will listen* (Grand Rapids, MI: Revell, 2008).

they are uncomfortable with face-to-face conversation, and they prefer to sit or stand next to their spouses.

Men talk about doing things and less about relationships. Even though men use their eyes, ears, and noses, women hear better, see better, and have a better sense of smell and touch and read emotions on a person's face more easily. A woman can pick nonverbal cues much more readily than a man. Johnson continues to say that for women, words over actions are important. Men are poor at expressing and identifying their feelings and are embarrassed to show their emotions. Men cannot talk, feel, and think at the same time; complaining or having problems is a sign of weakness.

The crucial point here is that, in many instances, the root of conflict in a relationship lies in the failure to comprehend these gender differences rather than the differences themselves being inherently problematic. It's important to note that while gender differences exist, there is a need to reject harmful gender stereotypes that can perpetuate misunderstanding and conflict in relationships. A very familiar expression Africans use to describe women is that women are weaker vessels, a reference to 1 Peter 3:7. However, Peter's use of "weaker partner" does not suggest a stereotype, that is, a demeaning or condescending characterization of women. Rather, he is raising the bar to suggest that the "responsibility for the husband is no less demanding. His assignment is to live with his wife, knowing her needs, recognizing her strengths and weaknesses, and treating her with 'honor' (*timen*, Gk.)—a term used to describe the value of a precious stone. Thus, she is to be treasured, reassured, protected, and loved, with every tender provision being made for her. If the husband fails in this mandate, he may find his prayers 'hindered.' The Greek term may be rendered 'cut off.'"[66] Perhaps we can consider the irony of a "weaker vessel" as sustaining a nine-month pregnancy and going through the birthing experience.

---

[66] William Macdonald, *The Believer's Study Bible*, WordSearch 11 online edition, accessed April 11, 2019. See also his discussion on *Believer's Bible Commentary* (Nashville, TN: Thomas Nelson, 1995), pp. 2268-2269.

The table below shows masculine and feminine stereotypes that should be overcome, according to Carolyn Schrock-Shenk.[67]

MASCULINE	FEMININE
Aggressive	Passive
Competitive	Cooperative
Rational	Irrational
Providers	Housekeepers
Express Power through Violence	Express Power through Communication
Independent	Dependent
Strong	Weak
Leaders	Followers

Table 1. Gender Stereotypes

These genuine male-female differences can very easily become the seedbed of stereotypes. Instead of embracing our God-given differences, we allow cultural gender attitudes to get the worst of us.

Unbalanced Approach to Likeness and Uniqueness

Linked to the differences in identity between men and women is the concept of identity likeness and uniqueness in all individuals. It's crucial to recognize that despite differences, all human beings share the same fundamental needs. When the aspects of likeness and uniqueness are not addressed in a balanced manner, it can lead to conflicts in relationships, particularly within the family dynamic. Striking a balance in acknowledging both commonalities and individual uniqueness is essential for fostering harmony in relationships.

David Pollock, Ruth Van Reken, and Michael Pollock discuss this

---

[67] Carolyn Schrock-Shenk, ed., p. 114.

matter of human identity from the prism of cross-cultural mobility and third-culture children. In their book, *Third Culture Kids*, they talk about what it means to be human.[68] They suggest that being human means being *relational* (being social), *emotional* (expressing feelings), *creative* (thinking and skills), *volitional* (choosing), *physical* (body), *spiritual* (spirit), *significant* (having value and purpose), and *integrated* (parts working together). The point they make here is that all human beings have these needs regardless of where they come from. Therefore, human beings have this common likeness.

However, this alone does not fully define human identity. The other side of the coin is that even though we share likeness, "we are not switchable beings." We also have differences (uniqueness). We come from different backgrounds and cultures that don't allow us to approach things the same way. We don't eat the same food, relate the same way, talk the same language the same way, look physically the same way, process information the same way, or express our feelings the same way. Everybody is unique. The big question, of course, is what one chooses to highlight as being the most important: likeness or uniqueness? Terminal uniqueness is when someone uses differences to isolate themselves with the notion that nobody understands them. This cave mentality results in dysfunctional relationships in the family.

Cognitive Dissonance Between Belief and Behavior

Cognitive dissonance occurs when there is a misalignment between belief and behavior. In relationships, couples may inadvertently communicate or act in ways that contradict their well-intentioned feelings. This discrepancy arises when individuals find themselves saying or doing the opposite of what they originally intended. In typical situations, an apology may follow such a "terminological inexactitude." If the spouse perceives it as a mistake, they may choose to overlook it. However, if this contradictory behavior becomes persistent and

---

[68] Pollock, Van Reken, and Pollock, pp. 104-107.

compulsive, addressing it promptly is crucial. If the issue persists, seeking therapy could be a beneficial option.

A story is told where children were fussing about what to have for breakfast. They came and stood around as Mother was getting their breakfast ready. When they saw the two packets of cereal on the kitchen counter, one of them asked, "Mom, which one of these packets is healthier?" The mother then pointed to one packet of cereal as the healthier one. But, pointing to the other packet of cereal, the children said: "We want this one." The fact is that even though the children knew which cereal was healthier, the preference was for the one that was less. That is what cognitive dissonance means. It happens when belief and behavior are not aligned. This is when you know what is right, but you consciously or willfully act differently.

Sometimes, the ego does not want to submit to humility and confession. You know that it is the right thing to apologize to your wife, but your masculinity (manhood) tells you, "Don't." It also happens in situations where you know that the results of what you do or say will be counterproductive. Instead of avoiding it, you still go ahead and do it anyway, regardless of the consequences. Paul, in Romans 7, expressed this same attitude or personal experience.

> "For we know that the law is spiritual, but I am carnal, sold under sin. [15] For what I am doing, I do not understand. For what I will to do, that I do not practice; but what I hate, that I do. [16] If, then, I do what I will not to do, I agree with the law that *it is* good. [17] But now, *it is* no longer I who do it, but sin that dwells in me. [18] For I know that in me (that is, in my flesh) nothing good dwells; for to will is present with me, but *how* to perform what is good I do not find. [19] For the good that I will *to do*, I do not do; but the evil I will not *do*, that I practice. [20] Now if I do what I will not *to do*, it is no longer I who do it, but sin that dwells in me. [21] I find then a law, that evil is present with me, the one who wills to do good. [22] For I delight in the law of God

according to the inward man. [23] But I see another law in my members, warring against the law of my mind, and bringing me into captivity to the law of sin which is in my members" (Rom. 7:14-23 NKJV).

As in Paul's case (Rom. 7:24-25), a way out of this dilemma is to make a conscious effort to submit to the will of Christ. Human effort without Christ is not sustainable. Christ overcame pride. In Philippians 2:5-8, Paul says, *"Let this mind be in you which was also in Christ Jesus, who, being in the form of God, did not consider it robbery to be equal with God, but made Himself of no reputation, taking the form of a bondservant, and coming in the likeness of men. And being found in appearance as a man, He humbled Himself and became obedient to the point of death, even the death of the cross"* (NKJV).

The expression "It's easier said than done" is often used to justify cognitive dissonance. In this case, the right thing to do is taken to be the ideal rather than the practical one. Use of this expression implies that some things are simply theoretical and not practical. In other words, knowing what to do is one thing, and doing it is another. Saying sorry to your spouse may be the right thing to do, but because of your ego, you decide not to apologize. Such an attitude shows a lack of transparency, openness, and authenticity, resulting in fracturing marital relationships.

Mismanaging Use of Power in Family Relationships

The term "power" in contemporary language often implies control and authoritative dominance. However, in this context, power is used to denote headship, leadership, authority, and expertise. Specifically regarding headship, the principle of male headship in the family is posited here. The power of headship is not about control but primarily about assuming ultimate responsibility, particularly in challenging situations. The head of the family functions as a shepherd, signifying the roles of provider and protector. Hence, the individual in this position must exhibit maturity and take charge when chaos emerges. Myles Munroe states:

> When you think about it, God really made only one human being. When He created the female, He didn't go back to the soil, but He fashioned her from the side of the man. . . Only the male came directly from the earth. This was because the male was designed by God to be the foundation of the human family. The woman came out of the man rather than the earth because she was designed to rest on the man - to have the male as her support.[69]

Male headship suggests management, not control or dictatorship. Male role is like that of a quarterback in football or a midfielder in soccer. A weak link between the defense and the offense costs the team a game. The quarterback's or midfielder's role is to ensure that the defense is not put under stress because of a weak link. Also, he distributes the ball to the offense in the front to put the opponent under stress.

Likewise, the role of male headship in the home involves setting the atmosphere for the rest of the family to function effectively in their respective roles. However, it's essential to recognize that power in the home is not exclusive to the man alone. Every family member, including children, holds varying levels of power crucial for the family's functioning. Power distribution fluctuates among individuals and changes in accordance with different stages of the family's development. For instance, the father's exercise of power may diminish as he ages. The use of power adapts and shifts to meet the evolving needs and situations within the family.

Power can also be assigned to a member of the family who has professional skills or expertise in each area that is needed in the family. Relying on that member is a wise thing to do. It is common among

---

[69] Myles Munroe, p. 38

African families for the husband to be in control of finances regardless of the financial skills he has. If the wife has professional skills or is a good financial manager, for strategic reasons, family financial management should be in her direction. Failure to understand and recognize these power patterns can cause family friction. A study by P. G. Herbst[70] observed behavioral relationships between spouses to determine (1) who does various group activities (2) who is the source of authority in each case, and (3) how much disagreement exists about it. The first two examined the social climate, while the third looked at the overt tension in the family group (husband and wife).

Herbst's study further showed three divisions of household duties (1) husband's household duties, (2) wife's household duties, and (3) common household duties. Herbst, however, cautioned: "It is clearly not sufficient merely to know who makes the decisions within a certain area of activity without also knowing the direction of the power relationship, that is, whose behavior is being decided about."[71] For this reason, power in the family is defined as "the ability of one family member to change the behavior of the other family member."[72] Power is understood as a system within the family rather than a personal characteristic. It is also understood to be an interactive process where family members react to power attempts. This reaction leads to another reaction, and so forth. The result of Herbst's study[73] is diagramed below:

Diagram 2: Family Patterns of Power

1. He decides and does the activity.

(Husband Autonomy)

---

[70]   P. G. Herbst, "The Measurement of Family Relationships," Sage Social Science Collections, 5 vols. (1), February 1952.

[71]   Ibid., p. 8.

[72]   Olsen, DeFrain, and Skogrand, p. 206.

[73]   Herbst, p. 9.

2. She decides and does the activity.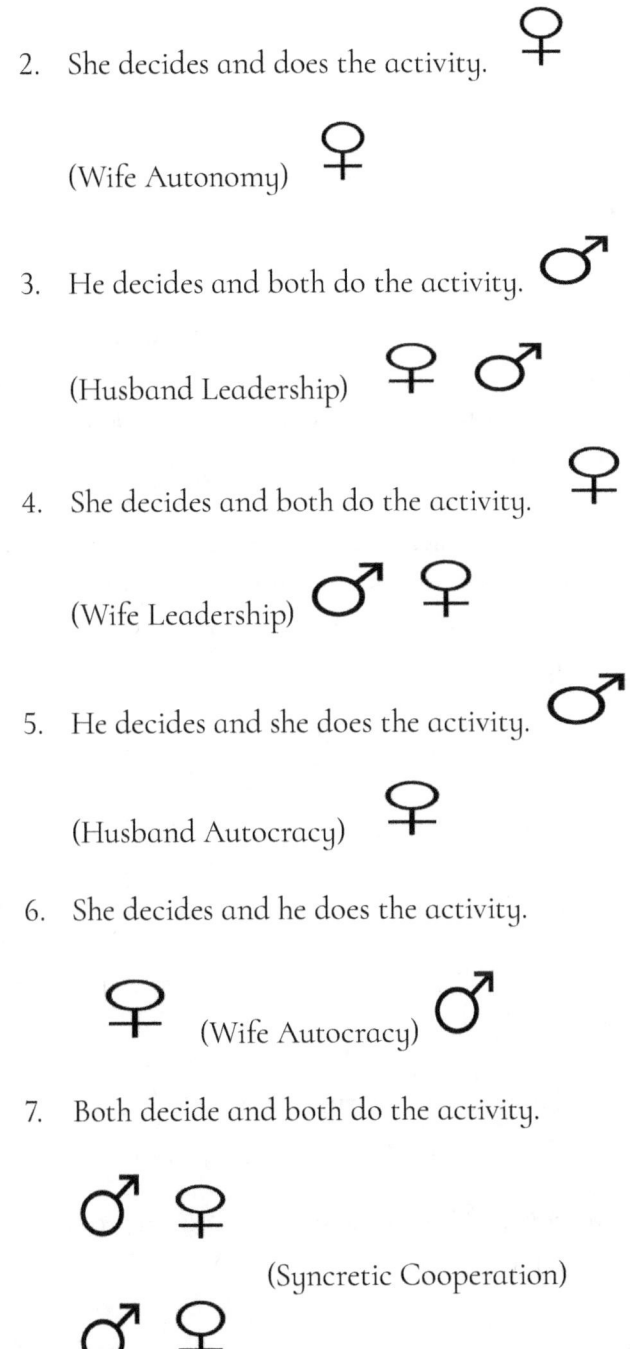

   (Wife Autonomy)

3. He decides and both do the activity.

   (Husband Leadership)

4. She decides and both do the activity.

   (Wife Leadership)

5. He decides and she does the activity.

   (Husband Autocracy)

6. She decides and he does the activity.

   (Wife Autocracy)

7. Both decide and both do the activity.

   (Syncretic Cooperation)

8. Both decide but he or she does the activity.

(Syncretic Div. of Function)

In the scenarios presented above, we notice that the distribution and utilization of power in marriage can be tied to factors such as financial standing, educational attainment, occupational prestige, intelligence, sociability, diverse life skills, social standing, sense of humor, and interpersonal abilities. The negotiation of power within family dynamics is a crucial element that can impact the relationship's stress levels. Challenges arise when one member consistently seeks to dominate decision-making. Olson and others propose six types of power within the family:[74]

> *Legitimate power.* The right to make decisions, as in the case between parent and child.

> *Reward power.* The ability to reward good behavior as a parent to a child.

> *Coercive power.* The ability to punish bad behavior, as a parent would to a child.

> *Referent power.* Having other's trust, that is, being recognized as trustworthy.

> *Informational power.* Having specialized knowledge in a particular area of concern.

---

[74] Ibid., pp. 208-209.

> *Expert power.* Having experience, skill, and respect in a particular area.

As the above list shows, no one individual in the family wields all the power; if one did, then the result is control or dictatorship. When power shifts during a conflict, sometimes a family member may demonstrate that power through violence.[75] This happens when the family member feels he or she is losing the power or that he or she has the power to control or dictate.

It's essential to emphasize that when addressing violence, the cultural context should be considered before addressing the violent act itself. Different social contexts may interpret violence in ways that deviate from conventional understanding. Overlooking the social context would be akin to applying a bandage without first cleaning the wound. Although violent behavior is unequivocally objectionable, it is crucial to comprehend the underlying reasons behind such conduct. This approach allows for a more nuanced understanding and facilitates the development of more effective solutions.

Associated with power is how that power is negotiated. This begs discussion about the decision-making process. Decision-making process is directly linked to the use of power. It prevents the use of power from becoming manipulative and authoritarian. The decision-making process, according to Turner and West, includes (1) reference or deference to persons with authority and status, (2) using rules to guide the discussion, (3) basing decisions on established values in the family, (4) use of discussion and consensus to arrive at a decision, and (5) de facto decisions—failure to decide.[76]

In fact, de facto decisions are not always bad. Back in the summer of 1995, Peggie graduated from Andrews University with her M.A. degree, eighteen months after being away from me (Zebron) and the children in Zimbabwe. Fortunately, I was able to attend her graduation. But then she decided to pursue a PhD that would take

---

[75] Turner and West, pp. 144-145.
[76] Ibid., pp. 160-162.

the next 3-5 years. We didn't think it was a good idea for the family to be separated that long. Joining her meant resigning from my job at Solusi University, not knowing what I would do in the United States. We talked back and forth about this until the night before I was due to fly back to Zimbabwe.

Despite the civil nature of the decision-making process, we ultimately reached no conclusion other than agreeing not to decide. A few days after my arrival in Zimbabwe, while driving with the two children in the car, jet lag overcame me. The next thing we knew, the car veered off the road, flew over rocks, and eventually crashed into shrubs and bushes. Thankfully, we emerged unscathed, but the car was completely wrecked. Arguably, we interpreted the accident as a sign for us to leave and return to the United States, which we eventually did. This experience underscores that the failure to decide can sometimes be a crucial element of the decision-making process. It is not always a detrimental idea, despite common perceptions.

Maleness Syndrome

It is common for some African males (husbands/fathers) to desire to assert authority. In Zulu/Ndebele, the expression "*Uzakungena esikhwameni*" literally means "your wife will enter into your pocket." This expression suggests that if you allow your wife to have her way in some matters, she will end up disrespecting you or taking you for granted. This suggests that a husband must maintain a safe and calculated distance from all the members of the family to preserve his status, power, and dignity. This attitude promotes the notion that being the man of the house means maintaining a certain psychological and emotional distance from your spouse and children.

Some African men find it demeaning to say to their colleagues, "Let me first talk to my wife, and I'll get back with you on this." They feel that doing so undermines their leadership position and gives power to the wife to make the decision. As a result, they make independent decisions that adversely affect their families. The irony is that husbands dread being alone. They cannot survive living without their wives, even though they don't want to publicly admit it. They have a hard time managing the anxiety and tension created by self-distancing and the desire to connect with the family. Unfortunately, they also refuse to seek counsel for the same reason of maleness.

Closed Family System and Inflexible Boundaries

Closed family systems contribute to the breakdown of some marriage and family relationships. In Africa, there's a common saying that anything occurring within the family should remain within its confines. This perspective is employed to emphasize the value of privacy. African culture often frowns upon whistle-blowers, discouraging abused family members from disclosing matters to individuals outside their immediate family. Due to the fear of blame or victimization, victims and other family members may be reluctant to report incidents to external parties. Consequently, such behavior tends to persist within the closed family system.

In an extended family system, conflicts are pervasive, marked by jealousies, competition, gossip, and disagreements among family members across generations. Strict warnings are issued within one household, prohibiting communication with members of another extended household regarding family matters. This practice aims to prevent leaks perceived as betrayals of one's family. While some level of privacy is expected for each family, obstructing whistle-blowers becomes a serious concern. This reluctance to report mistreatment results in victims and witnesses fearing to seek help, leading many instances of abuse to remain concealed until reaching a critical, often irreversible, point.

This brings in the matter of professional counseling, especially among families in the diaspora. In Western cultures, marriage is between two grown-up people who don't have to get parental consent to get married. However, the case is different among African communities. The extended family system rejects private marriages. The two who get married are also marrying each other's family. This means that when resolving conflicts, a counselor should consider the influence landed by the extended family system. It is understood that such a move may sometimes appear to compromise confidentiality. This dilemma often creates crises in marital counseling among diaspora families. A counselor needs to know the African context of marriage to diagnose the real issues affecting the African family. Marriage relationships are like spaghetti; they are complex and make it difficult for an outsider to get involved and help resolve the problem. Failure to reckon with this cultural perspective can exacerbate the conflict and result in divorce. Hence, George Allan Phiri observes that the current pastoral counseling training in Africa lacks the African cultural context to develop an African model of pastoral counseling.[77]

Lack of Sleep

A significant number of Africans in the diaspora grapple with sleep deprivation. As previously discussed, many of them engage in multiple jobs to provide for their families and fulfill various commitments, leading to a sleep duration of less than seven hours per day. Research indicates that insufficient sleep serves as the foundation for numerous health issues, including diabetes, heart disease, dementia, strokes, delayed recovery from injuries, and more. Regrettably, the prevailing norm involves excessive work hours and overtime.

A study by Michael Finkel says that sleep is essential for maintaining a healthy immune system, body temperature, and blood pressure. He states that sleep is more important than food and that a person will die faster due to lack of sleep than to lack of food.[78] In deep sleep our cells produce most growth hormones needed throughout life to service bones and muscles. Michael Frinkel states:

> Anyone who regularly sleeps less than six hours a night has an elevated risk of depression, psychosis, and stroke. Lack of sleep is also directly tied to obesity:

---

[77] George Allan Phiri, p. 122.
[78] Michael Frinkel, *The Science of Sleep: Want to fall asleep? Read this story*. National Geographic (August 2018), p. 66.

> Without enough sleep, the stomach and other organs overproduce ghrelin, the hunger hormone, causing us to eat more than we need. . .[79]

Insufficient sleep jeopardizes the well-being of families, leading them to allocate their hard-earned income towards medical expenses. To mitigate these costs, health insurance becomes essential, especially for those residing in the United States. Health insurance premiums can be substantial, even with workplace coverage assistance. From both financial and health perspectives, obtaining adequate sleep plays a crucial role in promoting overall well-being and preventing stress within family relationships.

There's another effect of undersleep that is often ignored. Studies show that under-slept individuals are more "irritable, moody, and irrational."[80] Lack of sleep affects every cognitive function. This implies that less sleep affects decision-making and can cause strange behaviors that often result in crime. Conflicts are more likely to occur when members of the family are mentally and physically tired. Sadly, lack of sleep is hardly addressed as a factor in hurting family relationships.

According to Dr. Matthew Walker, professor of neuroscience, psychology, and psychiatry, sleep-deprived individuals generate fewer and less accurate solutions to work-relevant problems they are challenged with.[81] He further states:

> Under-slept employees are not only less productive, less motivated, less creative, less happy, and lazier, but they are also more unethical . . . The less an individual sleeps, the more willing to lie to get free raffle tickets . . . Ethical deviance linked to a lack of sleep also weasels its way onto the work stage in a different guise, called social loading . . . Sleepy employees therefore choose the more selfish path of least resistance when working in

---

[79]   Ibid., p. 72.
[80]   Ibid.
[81]   Matthew Walker, *Why We Sleep* (New York: Scribner, 2017), p. 299.

teams, coasting by on the disingenuous ticket of social loading.[82]

Dr Walker makes a stunning observation: "Under-slept employees are not, therefore, going to drive your business forward with productive innovation."[83]

As we have seen, sleep deprivation negatively affects our health, our work ethic, and our social life. A case can be made that African families in the diaspora that work around the clock to make ends meet are highly at risk in all areas—health, work, and social life.

Involuntary Childlessness

According to Stephen J. Shaw's research, there's a general decline or plateau in birth rates in several countries on three continents.[84] In an interview by Jordan B. Peterson, Stephen Shaw described people who delayed their parenthood because they did not want children to interfere with their personal freedom to the point that some governments were even offering incentives for families to have more children.

Shaw observed that 30-40 percent of women desired to have children, while five percent of women didn't want children. The contributing reason Shaw found was that many women and men spent their earlier years acquiring an education and establishing a career path. Later in life, they experienced grief and suffering because of not finding a life partner or, in the case of women, their fertility window closed before them. Conversely, grief and pain were inflicted on those who made a choice not to have children by governments offering incentives to have children.

While Shaw's study described general trends of childlessness around the world, our focus here is on the impact that involuntary

---

[82] Ibid., p. 301.
[83] Ibid., p. 300.
[84] Stephen J. Shaw, "The Epidemic that Dare not Speak Its Name", an online interview by Jordan B. Peterson, March 2023, accessed on July 23, 2023.

or unplanned childlessness has on African families, particularly those living in the diaspora.

The societal expectation for couples to have children soon after marriage is a common belief in many cultures, not limited to Africans. The pressure to fulfill the biblical command to be fruitful and multiply, as mentioned in Genesis 1:28, is a shared sentiment across various communities. This cultural and religious expectation can indeed create a sense of urgency for newlyweds to start a family promptly. It's essential to recognize that each couple's journey to parenthood is unique, and societal expectations should be balanced with an understanding of the diverse factors that can influence family planning.

This view creates an irresistible sense of shame and insecurity, especially for the wife. Parents on both sides do not make it easy for the couple either. They always intimate or indirectly ask the couple when they plan to have children. If the couple tells them that they don't plan to have children, the folk will remind them that the Bible says to multiply and fill the earth. In fact, parents and families on both sides eagerly wait to have grandchildren and will often tell the couple that they would not want to die before they see their grandchildren. Aunts and the rest of the extended family have the same anticipation, even though not commonly expressed. The young wife is constantly under surveillance for any signs of pregnancy.

The pressure to have children can have severe psychological effects on a couple. In many African cultures, infertility is often associated with shame, particularly for the man who may feel a diminished sense of manhood. This societal perspective can lead to destructive behaviors, such as seeking to prove one's fertility through relationships outside of marriage. Traditional views also stigmatize women for infertility, sometimes resulting in additional marriages or divorces. Paradoxically, individuals who faced infertility in previous marriages might go on to have children in subsequent marriages, highlighting the complex and often unfounded nature of societal expectations.

Weaver, Revilla, and Koenig observe that in some cases, infertility is a result of sexual dysfunction, and in this case, a therapist would help the couple understand that their emotional needs are just as important as the goal of having a child.[85]

The sense of shame that an African woman sometimes feels is collaborated in Genesis 16. Abraham had been promised that he would become the father of many nations (Gen. 12:1-2). As time went by, Sarah and Abraham took matters into their own hands. Sarah initiated and orchestrated a plan to have her maid, Hagar, bear a child with Abraham. Under pressure, he succumbed, and Ishmael was born. It was common in Bible times (as was in Africa) to use surrogates for the sake of having children. Of course, things didn't always turn out to be a blessing to the trio. Hagar and her son had to leave. This Bible story is a good example of the power of culture in Bible times and in African societies.

The societal pressure and expectations regarding childlessness can indeed place significant stress on individuals, particularly women, within certain cultural contexts. The fear of not being fully accepted or facing judgment due to childlessness can be emotionally challenging for couples. It's crucial for societies to foster understanding and empathy toward couples facing difficulties in having children, recognizing that there are various factors influencing fertility. Encouraging open communication, support networks, and providing resources for couples dealing with fertility issues can contribute to healthier perspectives on marriage and family. Emphasizing the completeness of a marriage, regardless of whether it includes children, is an essential mindset shift.

Another contentious belief is not just the question of not having children but of not having boys. Traditionally, African marriages valued boys more than girls because boys perpetuated the family's name. It was believed that girls only brought in dowry but did not perpetuate the family's name. For that reason, the couple continued to have children until a boy was born. If this did not happen, an extra-marital affair would be the answer to the problem. There are still pockets of African communities that still hold onto this mindset.

---

[85] Andrew J. Weaver, Linda A. Revilla, and Herold G. Koenig, *Counseling Families Across the Stages of Life*, p. 198.

It is unfortunate that this kind of thinking exists even among some Christians.

Competing Dreams and Despair

The pursuit of dreams and goals, especially in the competitive environment of a new country, can indeed place stress on couples and families. Balancing individual aspirations with the practical realities of limited resources, time constraints, and external pressures can be challenging. It's essential for couples to engage in open communication, mutual support, and collaborative decision-making to navigate such challenges successfully. Additionally, seeking assistance from support networks, community resources, and counseling services can provide valuable insights and help maintain the well-being of the family unit.

John M. Gottman raises the most existential questions:

> Can people support one another in their life dreams? Can they develop a common sense of purpose, values, and mission that makes this brief journey of ours through life mean something? Can they really create, in this family, a new culture . . . that works? Marital therapy has failed in large measure because it hasn't examined the existential meaning of the most gridlocked issues—what we call the dream within the conflict.[86]

This echoes the words of Jesus: *"And if a house is divided against itself, that house cannot stand"* (Mark 3:25 NKJV). Perhaps the best way to resolve a conflict over competing dreams is the story, though fictional, of two goats trying to pass each other on a very narrow overpass. The two goats going opposite directions met at a mid-point on this narrow overpass. Since they could not pass each other or turn around, they stood there facing each other. After staring at each other for a very long time,

---

[86] John M. Gottman, *Why do fools fall in love?* p. viii.

they were getting hungry and tried to find a way out of their dilemma. Finally, one of the goats decided to kneel and let the other goat walk over it. That ended the stalemate, and each goat was on its way.

The concept of compromise and negotiation is crucial in maintaining a healthy and sustainable relationship, particularly when individuals within a couple have competing goals or dreams. Balancing personal aspirations with the shared objectives of the relationship requires effective communication, empathy, and a willingness to find common ground. As rightly pointed out, prioritizing and sequencing goals can be a strategic approach to managing conflicting objectives. Couples who actively engage in compromise and negotiation often build stronger and more resilient relationships.

When a goal is not achieved, the couple then turns weapons against each other and accuses each other of the failure. Such failures may lead couples to regret leaving their homeland to face such seemingly insurmountable challenges in the diaspora. In the book of Exodus, the Israelites left Egypt, the land of slavery, to the land of Canaan, a land that flowed with milk and honey. The analogy of the Israelites' journey and the challenges they faced resonates with the experiences of many individuals and families in the diaspora. Navigating a new life in a foreign land can indeed be challenging, and the longing for the familiar can be strong during difficult times. A strong sense of purpose, a unified family goal, self-discipline, patience, contentment, and faith, are valuable attributes that can help individuals and families overcome challenges and adapt to their new environment. The journey in the diaspora often requires resilience and a commitment to the shared vision for a better future.

Collapse of Traditional Guardrails

Years back, the home and the family were centers of power. Parents and guardians were responsible for nurturing their children. The church and the school were seen as an added layer of support. Primary responsibility lay in the hands of the family. A stable and strong family needs both parents to play their part in raising kids. Today, however, things have changed. The home, as the center, has lost its edge as more and more children are born and grow up under the care of single parents due to many factors.

The family's primary role has been delegated to the church and school, leaving them responsible for tasks originally assigned to the family. The failure to recognize the family's central role is now blamed for the challenges faced by young people. The church and school were meant to complement, not replace, the family's influence. In our postmodern society, there's a tendency to look to the government and politicians to address the issues facing young people. Despite allocating resources, the results are often unsatisfactory. A paradigm shift is necessary to refocus on the family and restore its central role, or the battle for the well-being of young people will continue to be challenging.

Shift from Abstinence to Pregnancy Prevention

Today's society has shifted emphasis from teaching the virtue of abstinence from premarital sex (chastity, moral purity) to pregnancy prevention. On one hand, sex before marriage is taken as a norm—leaving the family, the church, and the school out of the conversation. On the other hand, society is open to the phenomenon of singles moving in together and moving out at will. This is why pregnancy prevention is in high demand, keeping the pharmaceutical industry highly profitable.

In most young people's minds, high school dating and sex are attached; they go together. This shift in thinking and emphasis also opens the door to the use of controlled substances, condoms, and other pregnancy prevention options.

As far as the abortion issue is concerned in the United States, there is controversy about personhood and quality of life. There is also controversy among utilitarian (pro-abortion), pro-life, and abortion ban proponents over the termination of pregnancy. The utilitarian position focuses on outcomes and consequences, among other things; that is, whatever brings greater happiness to society (not the individual) is good. In other words, the end justifies the means. If the outcome is greater than the means of getting it, then the act is not inherently bad.

Proponents of prolife center their argument around stages of human development—sperm, zygote (conception), embryo, fetus, infant, child, youth, and adult.[87] They argue that from stage 4, abortion is wrong on moral and ethical grounds. The most religiously and politically charged position is that of banning abortion altogether. Proponents of this position demand the shutting down of abortion clinics in states where they have political control. African families are thus left to navigate these positions using Biblical principles.

Infotech and Biotech Advances

The Covid 19 pandemic changed everything. The use of technology, particularly interactive media, became a normal way of connecting with the outside world when formal gatherings became impossible. Technology has made interactions a lot easier. People were able to hold meetings virtually without having to travel or be in a physical space together at the same time. The blessing that came out of this was unimaginable.

However, Yuval Noah Harari cautions that "humans were always far better at inventing tools than using them wisely."[88] He argues that while technology results in mass unemployment, the shift in authority from humans to computer algorithms "is a much scarier scenario."[89] He fears the disintegration of free will as we lose control over our lives. Further, he is concerned about the daily encounter with "institutions, corporations, and government agencies that understand and manipulate what was hitherto my inaccessible inner realm."[90] Computers understand our bodies much better than we do.

---

[87] Robertson McQuilkin and Paul Copan, *An Introduction to Biblical Ethics*, 3rd ed. (Downers Grove, Illinois: InterVarsity Press, 2004), p. 364.

[88] Yuval Noah Harari, *21 Lessons for the 21st Century* (London: Penguin Random House, 2019), p. 16.

[89] Ibid., p. 56.

[90] Ibid., p. 62.

The drawback of technology is the diminishing emphasis on physical contact. Even within the same household, people rely on various technologies for communication. Entertainment, once a communal activity, has evolved into an individualized experience. Family members no longer feel the need to watch the same TV show together or engage in shared activities. The prevalence of video games has replaced traditional parent-child interactions and outdoor play. Even within marriages, couples resort to using cell phones as their primary means of communication, contributing to compromised relationship-building. While electronic gadgets offer entertainment, information, and education, their advanced algorithms are adept at understanding human behavior, detecting emotions, and tailoring content to individual preferences. This level of surveillance raises concerns about privacy and marketing influence.

It is said that artificial intelligence (AI) is smarter than our brains. It reads our moods, feelings, and minds. It can precisely predict our next thoughts. This means human freedom is taken over by machines, and we become automatons. How far this will go, nobody knows because engineers are left to function at will. Their areas of concern are lawsuits when people suffer damages or injuries caused by their products.

Sweeping Waves of Drugs and Pornography

In this context, the term "drug" pertains to illegal and addictive substances causing chronic, relapsing, compulsive disorders with adverse effects on brain function. Examples of such drugs include cocaine, alcohol, marijuana (weed), nicotine (tobacco), methamphetamines (meth), heroin, and fentanyl. There are many reasons why many people are drawn to using such drugs. One study listed four reasons:[91]

> ➤ To feel good. To get an intense feeling of pleasure, relaxation, and satisfaction. These benefits are short-lived.

---

[91] Ibid.

➢ To feel better. They take these to relieve stress and anxiety.

➢ To do better. They feel the pressure to improve performance in school, at work, and in sports.

➢ To satisfy curiosity and social pressure. For young people, peer pressure is very strong, and resistance is often not sustainable.

African families in the diaspora are not exempt from the impact of such drugs. Children and youth are not the only ones affected; adults too.

Laura Lander, Jani Howsare, and Marilyn Byrne discuss the impact of substance use disorders on families and children. They observe that the family "remains the primary source of attachment, nurturing, and socialization for humans in our current society."[92] They point out that substance use disorders (SUDs) "negatively affect emotional and behavioral patterns from the inception of the family, resulting in poor outcomes for the children and adults with SUDs."

Further, they observe that each member of the family uniquely affects the individual using substances. Issues that family members experience include unmet developmental needs, impaired attachment, economic hardship, legal problems, emotional distress, and sometimes violence. Thus, treating only the individual with addiction is not adequate.

These authors suggest that solely focusing on treating the individual without considering the broader family context may restrict the effectiveness of treatment. Initially, it overlooks the devastating impact of Substance Use Disorders (SUDs) on family members who remain "untreated," with their potential support unrecognized by counselors or therapists. Moreover, when one family member is entangled in

---

[92] Laura Lander, Janie Howsare, and Marilyn Byrne, "The impact of Substance Use Disorders on Families and Children: From Theory to Practice." Department of Behavioral Medicine and Psychiatry, West Virginia University School of Medicine, Morgantown, West Virginia. Online. Accessed April 30, 2023.

substance use, the entire family is affected, warranting therapy for the entire family unit.

Apart from drugs, pornography poses a negative impact on families. Watching videos and movies or reading pornographic materials affects behavior because, as Scripture says, by beholding we become changed (2 Cor 3:18). In other words, whatever our eyes and minds focus on has the power to affect our actions positively or negatively.

Public and political discourse on pornography has yielded no solutions. There are those who argue that pornography is a civil rights issue. Sharon J. Pressner, in her book Free Speech Versus Civil Rights, says that pornography is a form of sex discrimination linked with rape, battery, sexual harassment, sexual abuse of children, forced prostitution, and female sexual slavery. [93]

Conversely, some argue in defense of freedom of speech and expression. They contend that any law prohibiting the use of pornography would be deemed an unconstitutional infringement on the right to free speech. According to this viewpoint, it would be unconstitutional to sue the producers and distributors of such materials. From their perspective, they maintain that little can be done to curb the use of pornography.

From a Christian point of view, the use of and exposure to pornography has no social or positive value. Obscene images do affect the mind and lead to destructive behavior. Pornography is as addictive as drugs. For that reason, pornography does not enhance character development or contribute to healthy family relationships.

In instances where marital sexual fulfillment falters, some spouses resort to pornography as a means of sexual release. This introduces children and young people to premature exposure to sexual practices before marriage. Regrettably, the media exacerbates the situation, providing unrestricted access to pornographic materials that defy parental control and personal accountability, particularly since the practice often occurs in private.

---

[93] See Sharon J. Pressner, "Pornography: Free Speech versus Civil Rights?" in Amitai Etzioni, *Rights and the Common Good* (New York: St Martin's Press, 1995), pp. 107-111.

We raise these issues here because African families in the diaspora are experiencing a sweeping wave of drug usage and pornography. When a child, youth, or adult is involved, it creates conflict, violence, and disunity in the home.

Lack of Biblical Thinking

The absence of a moral compass or what we term Biblical thinking represents perhaps the most profound challenge in family relationships. We delve into this issue extensively in the upcoming chapter. In summary, however, most African marriages in the diaspora fail due to the following reasons:

- ➢ Lack of information on strategies for healthy family relationships

- ➢ Unwillingness to adjust and modify traditional family roles

- ➢ Collision between cultural and market norms

- ➢ Lack of skills to preserve values and adapt methods

- ➢ Prioritizing roles above relationship-building

- ➢ Leaving the home front unguarded

- ➢ Lack of sexual fulfillment

- ➢ Dwelling on the past than on the future

- ➢ Using the past as a fallback mode rather than the future

- ➢ Failure to recognize male-female differences

- ➢ Unbalanced approach to likeness and uniqueness

➢ Cognitive dissonance between belief and behavior

➢ Mismanaging the use of power in family relationships

➢ Maleness syndrome

➢ Closed family system and inflexible boundaries

➢ Lack of sleep

➢ Involuntary childlessness

➢ Competing dreams and despair

➢ Collapse of traditional guardrails

➢ Infotech and biotech advances

➢ Sweeping waves of drugs and pornography

➢ Lack of Biblical thinking

The list provided is not exhaustive, and it underscores the significance of incorporating biblical thinking into problem-solving. Consequently, we dedicate an entire chapter to elucidate the importance of adopting biblical thinking in everyday life. This approach stands out as paramount in maintaining a marriage relationship that is not only happy and healthy but also characterized by holiness.

APPLICATION: Which underlying issues do you feel need to be addressed to enhance your marriage and family relationship?

Chapter 4

BIBLICAL THINKING

"Change of behavior does not change anything until there's a change of mind." Ron Rockey

This chapter continues the discussion in chapter three about the underlying reasons for the breakup of African marriages and families in the diaspora. Here, we dedicate a full chapter to biblical thinking, the absence of which we consider to be the major contributor to the breakdown of marriage relationships.

Failure to Apply Biblical Thinking in Everyday Life

According to Alfred Jones:

> People are different in fundamental ways. They want different things; they have different purposes, aims, values, needs, drives, impulses, urges. Nothing is more fundamental than that. They believe differently; they think, cognize, conceptualize, perceive, understand, comprehend, and cogitate differently. Thus, manners of acting and emoting, governed as they are by wants and beliefs, follow suit and differ radically among people.[94]

---

[94] Alfred R. Jones, *The Black Male's Survival Manual* (Pine Forge, PA: Family Outreach Publications, 1999), p. 56.

Therefore, it may appear ambitious to anticipate that everyone will engage in biblical thinking. Nevertheless, opting for biblical thinking is imperative. According to Michael G. Hasel, biblical thinking applies in academics and deserves serious consideration. "I dream that our entire educational curriculum will be based on a biblical foundation. That our courses in psychology, history, biology, business, and literature be taught from a foundation of biblical thinking and worldview."[95]

A worldview is a specific philosophy or mindset through which we perceive, structure, and conduct our lives. Our upbringing, life experiences, values, and habits significantly influence our worldview. We encourage African families to adopt a biblical perspective when it comes to marriage and family relationships.

A disclaimer is warranted here: Using the Bible does not automatically make what we do or talk about biblical. The notion that everything will automatically align when one thinks biblically is a misconception, as it requires the complementary application for things to fall into place. Biblical thinking is a road map, not a completed journey. In the words of Jiri Moskala, Dean of the Seventh-day Adventist Theological Seminary: "It is about thinking biblically on life in its whole spectrum . . . discovering the biblical worldview and applying it widely and systematically to all spheres of life."[96]

Biblical thinking sets us in line with the purposes of our Maker. The Bible must be allowed to reorganize the furniture of our minds and influence our outward behavior. It is ironic to think that biblical thinking is limited only to religious issues; it can be applied to everything we do. Life in its totality is an act of worship (Rom 12:1-2).

It is essential for biblical thinking to become our instinctive default mode. Our values, thoughts, actions, and feelings should be consistently guided by a comprehensive process of biblical thinking. The definition and enhancement of marriages and family relationships

---

[95] Michael G. Hasel, "My Dream for Seventh-day Adventist Education," Adventist World (February 2017), p. 9.

[96] Jiri Moskala, "Biblical-Theological Thinking: The Foundations for Transformational Ministry," an unpublished paper presented at Andrews University, Berrien Springs, Michigan, October 2013.

can be achieved when all individuals involved in a marital partnership embrace biblical thinking. Our appeal for such thinking is rooted in the fact that, from the outset, God instituted marriage. Therefore, it is logical to adhere to God's instructions regarding male-female relationships. We need to discover God's design on how to handle marriage and family relationships. According to Myles Munroe, the Bible presents us with fundamental principles regarding God's purposes for male-female relationships, as follows:[97]

> Adam and Eve were created to be different (male and female, Gen. 1:27). This suggests gender differences in a marriage relationship.

> Adam and Eve were created for fellowship with God and to be relational like Him in reflecting His love (Jn 4:24). It should be a God-centered relationship. When Adam and Eve fell out with God, it began a downward spiral of fallouts of relationships with God and man, man and woman, man and environment, between siblings, ethnic and racial groups. Our foundations did indeed crumble (Ps. 11:3).

> The relationship between man and woman should be like that of God and man. A man needs God's presence before he needs the presence of a woman. Man is not wired to function outside the presence of God. This is why God came to look for Adam and Eve; He was servicing His relationship with His creation.

> To discover the purpose of something, never ask the creature but the Creator, the Maker. This is why God asked Adam and Eve, "Who told you that you are naked?" (Gen. 3:11)

---

[97] Myles Munroe, pp. 17-32.

> ➤ Male and female were originally created to rule together and to function together equally. This equality was designed and instituted by God.[98]

The illustration below depicts the channels or spheres that become our default when we engage in problem-solving without employing biblical thinking. This tendency tends to occur instinctively and without conscious effort. Simply put, our approach to life's challenges is often influenced more by a non-biblical worldview than by the principles outlined in the Bible. For example, when deciding which school a child should attend, parents may easily choose a school based on their finances (economic sphere), the school's academic reputation (sociological sphere), or proximity (psychological sphere). No doubt these are important factors to base a decision on. However, from a biblical worldview, the parents can consider the education of the child based on the Bible and Christian moral values. The Bible then shapes the parents' priorities as they relate to the child's education.

For example, parents can use the parable of the two builders in Matthew 7:24-29 in deciding their child's education. In the parable, one man built his house on the sand. In the metaphorical tale of the two houses—one built on a weak foundation and the other on a sturdy rock—God and His word serve as the robust foundation upon which a child's education should be anchored. While we acknowledge that parents rightfully prioritize factors such as quality, proximity, and financial considerations in their children's education, our call is to emphasize the Bible as the primary starting point in decision-making, with other considerations integrated accordingly.

---

[98] Ibid., p. 45.

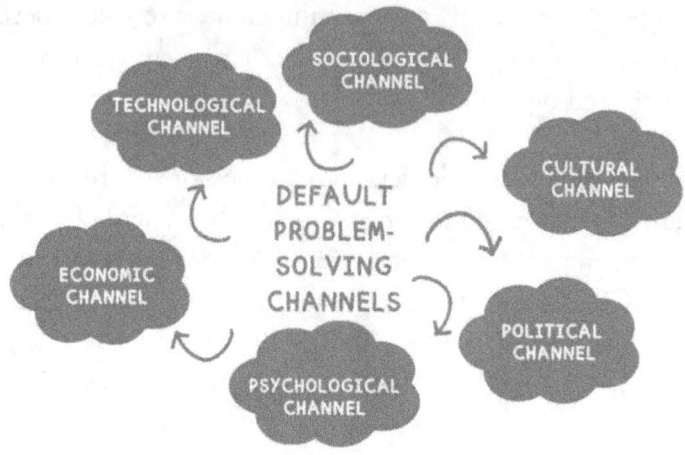

Diagram 3. Default Problem-Solving Channels

The depicted diagram illustrates various spheres or channels that individuals commonly turn to as their default when confronted with a problem. From our perspective, this represents a secular approach. Although human systems are operational, they may lack predictability and reliability. In Diagram 4 below, we present a more robust and superior approach to problem-solving. While acknowledging the role of human systems, this approach places the biblical thinking channel at the core, serving as the default in problem-solving.

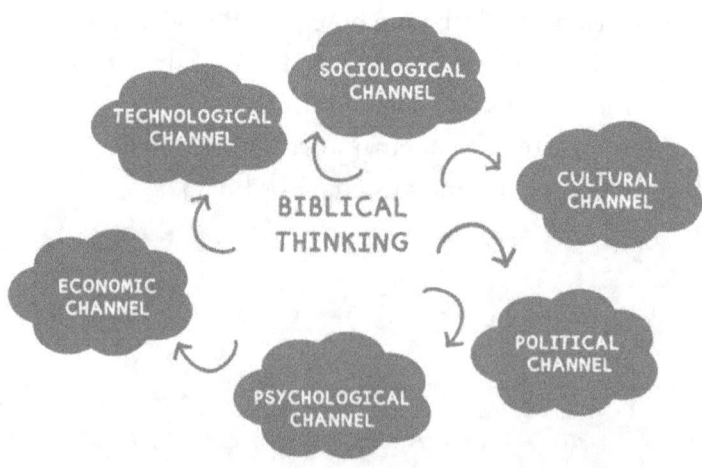

Diagram 4. Biblical Thinking and Problem-Solving

Biblical thinking is not intended to serve as a replacement for professional counselors, therapists, or other experts. Our standpoint is simply that adhering to Bible teachings fosters a lifestyle conducive to establishing healthy relationships for couples. In essence, a worldview and lifestyle rooted in biblical principles should contribute to couples interacting in a positive and wholesome manner. This positive transformation occurs because the Bible provides sound guidance on how to think, communicate, and behave with respect and responsibility. The Bible presents a lifestyle that is aligned with honoring God, offering timeless principles applicable in any cultural, ethnic, or geographical context. Its authority and finality derive from being the inspired Word of God.

Reverting to other channels (spheres) for problem-solving without any reference to the Bible puts one in a secular frame of mind. Matthew 6:33 says: *"But seek first the kingdom of God and His righteousness, and all these things shall be added to you"* (NKJV). For that reason, the Bible should be our primary source, and the other channels should be seen from the biblical perspective. Our stance emphasizes that while knowledge and insights from various disciplines or spheres hold significance, they should be approached within a biblical worldview. The Bible provides timeless principles that can be applied to address challenges in marriage and family life. Although the verses in the Bible originated in specific historical contexts, we can extract enduring principles that are relevant to our contemporary situations and contexts today.

As previously mentioned, the Bible is rich in principles and guidelines that couples can extract and apply when addressing issues that impact their marriage relationships. The following outlines how these principles can assist couples in adopting biblical thinking. Our preference and use of the New Living Translation (NLT) is simply for the purposes of clarity.

Biblical Relationship Principles

1. *"So stop telling lies. Let us tell our neighbors the truth, for we are all parts of the same body."* Eph. 4:25

   • <u>Principle</u>: Be truthful and honest

   • <u>Comment</u>: Honesty must go along with other values such as love, commitment, forgiveness, and godliness.[99]

2. *"Guard your heart above all else, for it determines the course of your life."* Prov. 4:23

   • <u>Principle</u>: Exercise judgment and self-discipline

   • <u>Comment</u>: Always keep your thoughts pure.

3. *"Gentleness, and self-control. There is no law against these things."* Gal. 5:23

   • <u>Principle</u>: Practice self-control

   • <u>Comment</u>: You can only control yourself, not your spouse.

4. *"Look! I stand at the door and knock. If you hear my voice and open the door, I will come in, and we will share a meal together as friends."* Rev. 3:20

   • <u>Principle</u>: Negotiate and respect

   • <u>Comment</u>: Don't force your way against the will of your spouse. Get enthusiastic support.

---

[99] Henry Cloud and John Townsend, *Boundaries in Marriage* (Grand Rapids, MI: Zondervan, 1999), p. 125.

5. *"And why worry about a speck in your friend's eye when you have a log in your own?"* Mat. 7:3

   - Principle: Repair your own fence first

   - Comment: Take ownership of your part of the issue and ask God to search your heart (Ps. 139:23-24).

6. *"I do not really understand myself, for I want to do what is right, but I don't do it. Instead, I do what I hate."* Rom. 7:15

   - Principle: Be reliable and consistent

   - Comment: We know what is right but choose to do what we know is wrong.

7. *"If another believer sins against you, go privately and point out the offense. If the other person listens and confesses it, you have won that person back."* Mat. 18:15

   - Principle: Practice reconciliation

   - Comment: Take the initiative; don't wait for the other person to take the first step. Jesus was the victim of our sins. He took the first step to reconcile us to Him.

8. *"The man replied, 'It was the woman you gave me who gave me the fruit, and I ate it.' Then the Lord God asked the woman, 'What have you done?' 'The serpent deceived me,' she replied. 'That's why I ate it.'"* Gen. 3:12-13

   - Principle: Blaming is condemning

   - Comment: Blaming each other is not a solution. Do not let your spouse's actions cause you to act sinfully. Don't cry victim, either. Don't throw each other under the bus when things go wrong.

9. *"Seek the Kingdom of God above all else, and live righteously, and he will give you everything you need."* Mat. 6:33

   • <u>Principle</u>: Put God first

   • <u>Comment</u>: Our connection with God is our primary purpose and source of blessings.

10. *"For we must all stand [appear] before Christ to be judged. We will each receive whatever we deserve for the good or evil we have done in this earthly body."* 2 Cor. 5:10

    • <u>Principle</u>: Focus on positives, not negatives

    • <u>Comment</u>: Let God be the ultimate judge of your spouse's motives.

11. *"If we claim we have no sin, we are only fooling ourselves and not living in the truth."* 1 Jn. 1:8; see also Rom. 3:10-18

    • <u>Principle</u>: Accept correction

    • <u>Comment</u>: Guard against self-justification. We all have a sinful nature.

12. *"If you think you are standing strong, be careful not to fall."* 1 Cor. 10:12

    • <u>Principle</u>: Be always diligent

    • <u>Comment</u>: Do not take your relationship for granted. Constantly work at it.

13. *"You must love the Lord your God with all your heart, all your soul, and all your mind. This is the first and greatest commandment. A second is equally important: Love your neighbor as yourself."* Mat. 22:37-39

- Principle: Pursue the mission of love

- Comment: Building relationships with God and one another is our very first mission. Loving God takes everything - our emotions, our being, our strength, and our mind).

14. *"Such love has no fear, because love expels fear. If we are afraid, it is for fear of punishment, and this shows that we have not fully experienced his perfect love."* 1 Jn. 4:18

   - Principle: Create an atmosphere of love

   - Comment: Love cannot exist in a climate of fear.

15. *"Do to others whatever you would like them to do to you. This is the essence of all that is taught in the law and the prophets."* Mat. 7:10

   - Principle: Be caring and sacrificial

   - Comment: Do what is right even if it causes you pain because when it is done to you, you will be happy.

16. *"Wisdom will save you from the immoral woman, from the seductive words of the promiscuous woman."* Prov. 2:16

   - Principle: Shun any appearance of evil

   - Comment: Be trustworthy. Shun bad company.

17. *"For a prostitute will bring you to poverty, but sleeping with another man's wife will cost you your life."* Prov. 6:26

   - Principle: Practice fidelity at all costs

   - Comment: Your spouse's unfaithfulness should not be an excuse for yours.

18. *"Most important of all, continue to show deep love for each other, for love covers a multitude of sins."* 1 Pet. 4:8

   • <u>Principle</u>: Love does not excuse the guilty

   • <u>Comment</u>: No failure is larger than love, but don't make excuses for your spouse's sins.

19. *Again, the Kingdom of Heaven is like a merchant on the lookout for choice pearls. When he discovered a pearl of great value, he sold everything he owned and bought it!"* Mat. 13:45-46

   • <u>Principle</u>: Value each other

   • <u>Comment</u>: Pearls don't lose or change their value; your spouse doesn't either.

20. *"Anyone who does the will of my Father in heaven is my brother and sister and mother."* Mat. 12:50

   • <u>Principle</u>: Create friendships

   • <u>Comment</u>: Marriage relationships need a village for support. Practice community.

21. *"If the whole body were an eye, how would you hear? Or if your whole body were an ear, how would you smell anything? But our bodies have many parts, and God has put each part just where he wants it."* 1 Cor. 12:17-18

   • <u>Principle</u>: Recognize your uniqueness

   • <u>Comment</u>: Our differences are not the problem. Our attitude toward them can be a problem that invites other problems.

22. *"As iron sharpens iron, so a friend sharpens a friend."* Prov. 27:17

   • <u>Principle</u>: Be open to criticism

   • <u>Comment</u>: When you take criticism, you come out better and stronger.

23. *"But I say that a man who divorces his wife, unless she has been unfaithful, causes her to commit adultery. And anyone who marries a divorced woman also commits adultery."* Mat. 5:32

   • <u>Principle</u>: Go the distance

   • <u>Comment</u>: God permits divorce conditionally but does not demand or mandate it. Divorce is a life-long stain; avoid it as much as you can.

24. *"Do you not know that your bodies are temples of the Holy Spirit, who is in you, whom you have received from God? You are not your own; you were bought at a price. Therefore honor God with your bodies."* 1Cor. 6:19-20

   • <u>Principle</u>: Practice self-care and respect

   • <u>Comment</u>: We must avoid sexual immorality, illicit behavior, and impure lifestyle.

25. *"Encourage those who are timid. Take tender care of those who are weak. Be patient with everyone."* 1 Thess. 5:14

   • <u>Principle</u>: Be supportive and patient

   • <u>Comment</u>: Always support your spouse; be available when your help is needed.

26. *"Or, what a miserable person I am! Who will free me from this life that is dominated by sin and death?"* Rom. 7:24

    - <u>Principle</u>: Change takes time

    - <u>Comment</u>: Don't expect your spouse to change overnight. Give your spouse time to change (Ezek. 3:18-19), except when abuse, drugs and alcohol are involved.[100]

27. *"Dear friends, never take revenge. Leave that to the righteous anger of God."* Rom. 12:19. *"See that no one pays back evil for evil, but always try to do good to each other and to everyone else."* 1 Thess. 5:15

    - <u>Principle</u>: Revenge is God's business

    - <u>Comment</u>: Do not take revenge against the one who hurt you. Instead, get help from people and places where you can heal and learn to solve the problem.

28. *"A good tree produces good fruit, and a bad tree produces bad fruit."* Mat. 7:17

    - <u>Principle</u>: Seek the root cause

    - <u>Comment</u>: The issue you are dealing with maybe just the fruit (symptom) of a deeper problem.

29. *"It is better to live alone in the corner of an attic [upper floor] than with a quarrelsome wife in a lovely home."* Prov. 21:9

    - <u>Principle</u>: Nagging drains love

    - <u>Comment</u>: Repeating the same argument or point over and over has never changed anyone.

---

[100] Ibid., p. 219.

30. *"Hot-tempered people must pay the penalty. If you rescue them once, you will have to do it again."* Prov. 19:19

    • <u>Principle</u>: Enabling wrongdoing stings

    • <u>Comment</u>: If you enable your spouse's behavior, you will only make it worse.

31. *"O Jerusalem, Jerusalem, the city that kills the prophets and stones God's messengers! How often I have wanted to gather your children together as a hen protects her chicks beneath her wings, but you wouldn't let me."* Mat. 23:37

    • <u>Principle</u>: Don't give up on each other

    • <u>Comment</u>: God grieves with us when we reject His love. He does not give up on us.

32. *"Come now let's settle this,' says the Lord. "Though your sins are like scarlet, I will make them as white as snow. Though they are red like crimson, I will make them as white as wool."* Isa. 1:18

    • <u>Principle</u>: No problem is too big to talk about

    • <u>Comment</u>: We must work things out together. Withdrawal and refusal to talk are abusive tendencies. Talking things over may include professional counseling.

33. *"Turn away from evil and do good. Search for peace, and work to maintain it."* 1 Pet. 3:11

    • <u>Principle</u>: Strive for peace

    • <u>Comment</u>: Create, initiate, and keep the peace. Stop anything that does not promote peace.

The Bible addresses every facet of our lives, including family and marriage relationships. While the previously mentioned principles don't encompass every possible scenario, they focus on illuminating the most common situations in marriage and family life. The Bible stands as a reliable resource that we can trust to navigate and resolve our problems. By embracing biblical thinking and adopting a biblical worldview, we position ourselves for success, even as we incorporate cultural contexts into our understanding.

APPLICATION: To what extent does biblical thinking compare with other thinking spheres in problem-solving?

Chapter 5

SMELLING OURSELVES

"There is no missionary field more important than the home." Ellen G. White

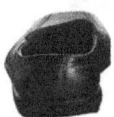

The union between husband and wife cannot be fully understood or explained. In the Bible, Paul attempts to explain it in reverse. He speaks of the relationship between Christ and the church as being analogous to the relationship between husband and wife (Eph. 5:21; Col. 3:18-19). In other words, the relationship between Christ and the church is best explained by understanding the relationship between husband and wife.

The analogy of the shoes, akin to Paul's metaphorical expression, is our attempt to elucidate the concept of spouses being one flesh. It's like both the husband and wife are donning one of their partner's shoes along with one of their own, walking in them comfortably. However, there's a static reality both must confront – they cannot alter their foot size to fit into the spouse's shoe, nor can they adjust the shoes to accommodate their own feet. This imagery of shoes underscores the importance of acknowledging the uniqueness and identity of everyone.

Nevertheless, the couple must exert effort to truly understand each other, delving into the reality of each other's worldview.

The process of getting to know one's spouse is often challenging and, at times, difficult. The Bible refers to it as "agape," signifying sacrificial love. Achieving this level of understanding requires a significant amount of self-discipline. Marriage is a school where God teaches us to know each other by wearing each other's shoes and not being bashful. To accomplish that, this chapter focuses on smelling ourselves. In Zulu, this literally means sniffing your own armpits. When you do that, you then realize that you are not perfect. It's often easier to recognize or smell another person's odor than your own. Marriages would be more sustainable if we learned how to smell ourselves, took responsibility for what goes on in the relationship, and accepted that we have a part to play in the situation.

The Johari Window

One way to smell ourselves is by using the concept known as the "Johari Window." It is a model that has been used widely to understand oneself. It is credited to Joseph and Harrington (hence Johari), who created the model to show the various stages of relational understanding and self-awareness.[101] The Johari Window has four panes (quadrants created by the intersection of a vertical and a horizontal line). Each pane (quadrant) represents an aspect of yourself, including things known and unknown to you. This is where self-disclosure or self-discovery takes place.

The window in diagram 5 below shows quadrants representing four aspects of you: open, blind, hidden, and unknown areas.

---

[101] Steven A. Beebe, Susan J. Beebe, Diana K. Ivy, *Communication: Principles for a Lifetime* (Boston, MA: Allyn and Bacon, 2001), 216.

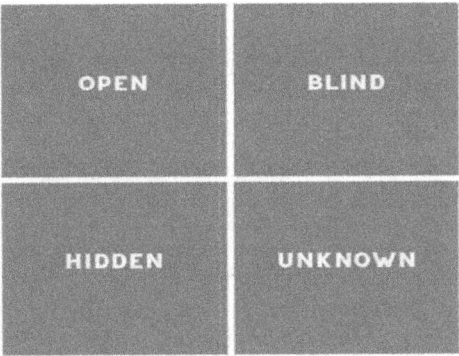

Diagram 5. Johari Windows

Explanation of Quadrants

Open Area. Most communication occurs in the open area where information about attitudes, behavior, emotions, feelings, skills, and views are shared. As Evan B. Howard says, "Revelation is built on self-disclosure."[102] As husbands and wives gain a deeper understanding of each other, the open areas in their relationship widen. This increased knowledge contributes to a more effective and dynamic connection between them. The growth in intimacy is heightened, fostering a greater likelihood of a healthy relationship.

Blind Area. Information about oneself can be known to others and remain unknown to the individual. Additionally, others might interpret someone differently than expected, and deliberate withholding of information may occur to protect feelings. To diminish the blind area, seeking feedback from one's spouse or others becomes crucial.

Hidden Area. There is information known to an individual but intentionally kept unknown to others. This is the realm where personal secrets are safeguarded—private information such as feelings, past experiences, fears, and undisclosed matters. Despite the impact on the marriage relationship, individuals often choose to keep certain feelings and information private. However, this practice can be detrimental

---

[102] Evan B. Howard, *The Brazos Introduction to Christian Spirituality* (Grand Rapids, MI: Brazos Press, 2008), p. 205.

to the relationship, particularly if the information is significant to the spouse or others involved. Therefore, it becomes essential to diminish the hidden area by safely sharing and moving the information into the open.

Unknown Area. The unknown area encompasses information that an individual is unaware of about themselves and others are also ignorant of, including feelings, capabilities, talents, and potentially even aspects related to past traumatic experiences. Discovery of these hidden qualities and capabilities can occur through self-observation or observation by others. As the unknown area decreases, there is an expansion of self-understanding, contributing to the growth of the marriage relationship.

When all four panes are of equal size, it indicates a constrained relationship with your spouse, lacking substantial self-disclosure. The reluctance to disclose information that would expand the open area hinders self-disclosure. In this scenario, the vertical line adjusts the size of each quadrant to the right or left, while the horizontal line adjusts it up or down. This implies that each area can either narrow or widen, depending on the choices made about opening up to others. As one quadrant enlarges, the adjacent one may narrow. It's worth noting that, upon closer inspection, the four quadrants form a sign resembling a cross. Some people may argue that it is through the cross that we gain a deeper understanding of ourselves and establish more meaningful connections with others.

Self-discovery and self-disclosure do not come easy. There are cultural myths that make the process more challenging. For example, in African culture, as in many cultures, it is expected that boys (men) don't show emotions such as crying publicly. If they do, they are seen to be exhibiting feminine characteristics, and that is perceived negatively. Certainly, societal expectations and cultural norms often influence how individuals handle self-disclosure. In the context of gender roles, men may avoid showing their emotions to uphold a perceived sense of manhood and preserve their ego.

Conversely, there might be cultural expectations for women to openly express their emotions, particularly through crying.

Paradoxically, despite these expectations, women may still be perceived as weak. The crucial point emphasized here is that one's upbringing significantly shapes their approach to self-disclosure. Cultural and societal norms play a substantial role in influencing how individuals express and share their emotions.

The willingness to open up and share personal experiences is closely tied to the level of trust between spouses. Self-disclosure inherently involves a certain degree of risk, and individuals are more likely to share when they feel safe and secure within the relationship.

In the early stages of a new marriage, it's common for all four quadrants to be relatively equal in size. As the relationship develops and trust deepens, individuals may feel more comfortable and secure, leading to adjustments in the size of the quadrants as self-disclosure becomes more prevalent.

As the level of freedom and trust develops, the size of the quadrants will each start to shift either by widening or narrowing. Widening means that husband and wife are allowing each other to come into their individual space and know more about them without being threatened. Narrowing means husband and wife don't feel comfortable sharing information about themselves because they don't feel safe, or the information may be used against them.

According to Morreale, Spitzberg, and Barge, the process of self-disclosure is more like a faucet than a light switch. With the typical light switch, the light is either on or off. But with a faucet, we can control water temperature, pressure, direction, and amount of water let out. Self-disclosure is a gradual process that takes place over time.[103]

The authors discuss four elements that are involved in self-disclosure: breadth, depth, value, and relevance. In self-disclosure, the individual decides or controls (1) how much to disclose, (2) what to disclose, (3) the risks involved, and (4) the relevance to the issue being discussed. Self-disclosure is complex; this is why trust is a key aspect of a marriage relationship.

---

[103] Sherwyn P. Morreale, Brian H. Spitzberg, and J. Kevin Barge, *Human Communication: Motivation, Knowledge & Skills* (Belmont, CA: Thomson Learning, 2001), pp. 76-79.

The Johari Window serves as a valuable tool for couples to explore individual self-discovery and recognize aspects that either foster or impede growth within their relationship. It shifts the focus away from blame and encourages each spouse to cultivate self-awareness and engage in self-disclosure. In essence, the Johari Window prompts each partner to view themselves as active contributors to the relationship rather than as victims. The key emphasis lies in redirecting attention from the spouse to oneself, fostering a more constructive and introspective approach to relationship dynamics. That is what it means to smell yourself. The Bible calls this self-control or self-discipline (Gal. 5:23). The concept of smelling ourselves discourages couples from spending a lot of their time blaming and pointing fingers at each other. Another way couples can smell themselves is by assessing their emotional needs.

Troubleshooting Check Sheet

Peggie and I (Zebron) got married at Andrews University in Michigan. We had to work to pay the bills. During the summer, I made sure that I did not schedule myself to work on Sundays so I could enjoy playing soccer, among other things. Peggie, instead, put more hours of work on Sundays than during the weekdays. I hadn't fully grasped the impact of the amalgamation of financial strain, academic stress, and my apparent lack of awareness of her emotional state. The irony of my enjoyment on the soccer field, while she worked long hours, became glaringly obvious. One day, she opened up and told me how she felt about the matter. Playing soccer was not necessarily the problem. It was my independent behavior and insensitivity to her stress that was the problem.

It was a surprising realization for me when Peggie put a lot of effort into cooking rice and beans, and, in gratitude, I would express appreciation for the "delicious meal." However, after enduring this for a while, I reached a point where I could no longer keep my true feelings bottled up. I eventually opened up to Peggie and honestly shared that although I appreciated her cooking, I had been eating under protest. I disclosed that my preferred food choice was cornmeal (*fufu, ugali, sadza, nsima*) with greens. She looked at me and then said: "All this time, you have been thanking me for the delicious meals when, in fact, you were not enjoying the food. Why did it take you so long for you to tell me this?" To say it was embarrassing is an understatement. By the way, while she cooks cornmeal and greens, she still cooks rice and beans, and I have learned to enjoy it.

Willard F. Harley, Jr. has done a lot of research and writing about romantic love and emotional needs between spouses. One of his great accomplishments is identifying six killers (love busters) of a relationship between husbands and wives: *selfish demands, disrespectful judgments, angry outbursts, dishonesty, annoying habits,* and *independent behavior.*[104] Clearly, in our case, the failure to share thoughts and feelings, likes and dislikes, as well as independent behavior, became a hindrance to our relationship. It wasn't until both of us felt able and comfortable to open up to each other that positive changes started to take place.

According to Harley, Jr., couples should use these six love busters as a troubleshooting check sheet to identify behaviors that destroy the quality of their relationship. We strongly recommend incorporating Harley's Love Busters as an additional method for couples to gain self-awareness. From our perspective, these Love Busters provide a comprehensive framework that addresses many destructive habits within marital relationships. Virtually all the complaints spouses may have against each other can be categorized under the umbrella of these Love Busters.

Have you noticed that every time you visit a doctor for the first time or after a very long time, the first thing you are asked to do immediately after checking in is answer to a lot of questions about your personal health. It's a long list of questions that cover a wide range of health issues that the doctor wants to know about you. When asked to share your health history and identify your health concerns, the assumption is that, as an individual, you possess some knowledge of your body. It's akin to standing in front of a mirror and being prompted to identify spots on your face. This analogy aligns with the

---

[104] Willard F. Harley Jr. *Five Steps to Romantic Love* (Grand Rapids, MI: Fleming H. Revell, 2002), pp. 19-28. See also, *Love Busters: Overcoming Habits That Destroy Romantic Love* (Grand Rapids, MI: Fleming H. Revell, 2002), pp. 49-160.

concept of "smelling ourselves." While Harley suggests that couples should evaluate each other, the idea is that you don't have to wait for your spouse to point out issues; you can proactively engage in self-awareness and reflection.

Another checklist that Harley, Jr. uses is one dealing with emotional needs. He makes the point that when couples meet each other's emotional or felt needs, it improves the quality of their relationship. He has identified ten emotional needs that every spouse wants met: *affection, conversation, recreational companionship, honesty and openness, attractiveness, financial support, domestic support, family commitment, admiration,* and *sexual fulfillment.*[105] These are identified as one's ability to care, that is, to make each other happy even when it hurts your ego. Both spouses must freely do this. Harley, Jr. clarifies what this means:

> Often, the failure of men and women to meet each other's emotional needs is simply due to ignorance of each other's needs and not selfish unwillingness to be considerate. Fulfilling those needs does not mean you have to painfully grit your teeth, making the best of something you hate. It means preparing yourself to meet needs you may not appreciate yourself. By learning to understand your spouse as a totally different person than you, you can begin to become an expert in meeting all that person's emotional needs.[106]

To this Cloud and Townsend concur: "We deny ourselves certain freedoms to say or do whatever we'd like in order to achieve a higher purpose."[107] Smelling ourselves may mean taking steps to check with your spouse how he/she feels about your behavior in each category of love busters and emotional needs. This means being willing to listen and accept each other's point of view because it is based on how both

---

[105] Willard F. Harley, Jr. *His Needs, Her Needs* (Grand Rapids, MI: Fleming H. Revell, 2001), pp. 36-165.

[106] Ibid., p. 19.

[107] Henry Cloud & John Townsend, p. 62.

of you feel. Denying your spouse's feelings is the worst that you can do for your relationship. It is important to ask your spouse for any suggestions on what you can do to make him/her feel differently.

Setting Boundaries

Indeed, many games are structured around the idea of winning rather than losing. In these games, players often strive to shift the problem onto the other side to secure a victory. For instance, in tennis, the player hits the ball back to the opponent, ensuring that the problem remains on their side of the court. This dynamic is mutual, with each player adopting a similar strategy. However, what works to win a game in tennis doesn't translate well to a marriage relationship. Marriage is not a game of tennis or ping-pong, where the goal is to leave the responsibility to the other person. In a healthy marriage, taking shared responsibility is crucial, and the "winning at all costs" mentality can be detrimental to the relationship.

Nedra Glover Tawwab defines boundaries as "expectations and needs that help you feel safe and comfortable in your relationships."[108] She further explains that "expectations in relationships help you stay mentally and emotionally well. Learning when to say no and when to say yes is also an essential part of feeling comfortable when interacting with others."[109] It "is a cue to others about how to treat you."[110] Tawwab underscores two things needed in setting boundaries: *communication* and *action*. First, boundaries must be communicated clearly and assertively. Second, you must uphold what you communicate through your behavior.[111]

The absence of boundaries often leads to inevitable conflict. Establishing boundaries is a way to manage what belongs to you, distinguishing it from what belongs to others. It's analogous to when you purchase a piece of land, and the title company provides a map that

---

[108] Nedra Glover Tawwab, *Set Boundaries, Find Peace* (New York: TarcherPerigee, 2021), p. 5.
[109] Ibid.
[110] Ibid., p. 9.
[111] Ibid., pp. 13-14.

delineates your property lines, not those of your neighbor. In essence, boundaries revolve around your responsibilities, not those of others.

Smelling yourself, in this context, involves recognizing and taking responsibility for what you own rather than attempting to control what belongs to others. It aligns with the life axiom that in every conflict, there is shared ownership. This implies active participation in problem resolution, even when it may seem that the fault lies with the other person.

Cloud and Townsend have done great work in this area of setting boundaries in marriage. They suggest that taking responsibility means taking ownership of our property lines to be good neighbors. In a marriage relationship, the property lines are defined by feelings, attitudes, behaviors, choices, limits, desires, thoughts, values, talents, and love.[112] It's crucial to note that setting boundaries doesn't involve dictating limits for your spouse; rather, it means marking your own yard for protection. This includes areas related to self-control, language, consequences, and values.

Each spouse is responsible for establishing and respecting these boundaries. There are instances where taking responsibility may necessitate emotional and physical distancing, particularly in cases of physical abuse. Boundaries play a significant role in maintaining a healthy and respectful dynamic within the marriage.

Emotional distance often occurs when a spouse has been unfaithful, as the breach of trust significantly impacts the relationship. It's crucial to bear in mind two key aspects: firstly, trust is something that must be earned. While the spouse who was unfaithful can be forgiven, it doesn't automatically restore the trust to its previous level. Rebuilding trust becomes a deliberate process, and the unfaithful partner needs to actively work towards earning that trust back. Forgiveness may pertain to a specific behavior, but trust is intricately tied to character and requires intentional effort to rebuild.

Unless the erring spouse's character changes, his/her behavior remains the same. This brings us to the second point: that earning trust

---

[112] Henry Cloud & John Townsend, 2010, p. 92.

takes time. The unfaithful spouse should not anticipate immediate trust simply by confessing and seeking forgiveness. It's crucial for them to recognize that rebuilding trust is a gradual process. The offended spouse can contribute to this process by offering the guilty party the opportunity to grow, improve, and ultimately regain the trust that was lost. Patience, understanding, and mutual effort are key components in the journey toward rebuilding trust after a breach in a relationship.

Physical distance can become necessary when other solutions fail, especially when the environment and atmosphere are not conducive to peace-making. In certain situations, creating a physical separation can provide the needed space for both parties to reflect, heal, and work towards resolution in a more suitable setting. When the situation is hostile, you may remove yourself from an argument or heated situation by taking any of the following steps (boundaries) depending on the nature of the problem or situation:

➢ Take time away from each other to sort things out.

➢ Move out to get treatment for an addiction.

➢ Separate from physical abuse or substance abuse immediately.

➢ Move into a shelter to protect yourself and your children.

➢ Seek counseling and support groups.

Indeed, cultural perspectives, including some in African societies, can often impose gendered expectations and norms on individuals, particularly in the context of infidelity. It's not uncommon for women to face societal pressure to accept male infidelity as a perceived norm or expected behavior. Cultural expectations may place an emphasis on forgiveness and the endurance of the relationship, even in the face of infidelity. These cultural norms can create challenges for women who may feel compelled to conform to societal expectations rather than asserting their own boundaries and seeking personal well-being. The negotiation between cultural expectations and individual needs can be complex and vary widely across different societies and communities. Another extenuating circumstance that forces a woman to stay in the relationship is the children's security. And yet, when tables are turned the other way, the infidelity of a woman is treated as shame, and the woman often merits immediate divorce.

What we are saying here is that the concept of smelling ourselves and setting boundaries is necessary for both husband and wife. The onus is on them to choose to deal with cultural expediencies that favor maleness and for them to follow biblical thinking instead. Such boundaries need to be communicated and established very early in the relationship rather than when a problem has developed. This presupposes the existence of freedom and self-control in the relationship and the absence of fear and control.

Indeed, establishing boundaries and communicating commitments in a relationship is often most effective when done during times of calm and normalcy rather than waiting until conflicts arise. This proactive approach allows both spouses to be in a better position to listen and understand each other's needs and expectations. The analogy with air hostesses communicating boundaries before a plane takes off is apt. Setting expectations and boundaries early on can help prevent misunderstandings and conflicts down the line, creating a foundation for a healthier and more resilient relationship. Waiting until conflicts have already surfaced can make it more challenging to establish clear boundaries and may lead to more complex and emotionally charged conversations.

APPLICATION: What would you say is your spouse's largest quadrant considering the Johari window? Any examples of self-disclosure that enhanced your marriage relationship?

CHAPTER 6

CONFLICT MANAGEMENT IN THE FAMILY

"Peace cannot be kept by force. It can only be achieved by understanding." Albert Einstein

As we get into the discussion about conflict management in the family, we need to understand the following premises:

➤ That conflict is inevitable when people share a close relationship.

➤ That conflict warns of danger, like traffic signals or symptoms of illness.

➤ That conflict, if not resolved, can set the stage for abuse, fights, separation, and divorce.

➤ That conflict is not necessarily evil; it is generally a function of caring. It happens when people care about each other and care about their interests, which they don't want to lose.

➤ That conflict, if resolved, promotes intimacy in marriage. Couples know each other better because they move from the superficial to the deeper levels of understanding and knowing each other.

➢ That conflict has many facets that need to be identified and handled prayerfully, skillfully, tactfully, and even professionally.

➢ That conflict is often misdiagnosed when couples attribute to it what it does not deserve. Disagreements and arguments do not always mean there's conflict.

➢ That conflict can provide necessary changes, helping us mature in relationships.

Conflict is a subject that frequently comes up in marriage seminars and counseling sessions. Understanding conflict in its broader context, especially within the framework of marriage and family, is crucial. Resolving conflicts involves the essential step of identifying the nature or specific area of the conflict since effective solutions can only be applied to what is accurately identified and defined. This is why doctors use X-rays and CAT scans to diagnose the problem to treat it. Like sickness in the human body, conflict in marriage and family is a result of several causes, such as goals, preferences, standards, values, and culture. As has already been said above, disagreements do not necessarily suggest there's conflict.

Conflict Managing Styles

Good conflict management does not necessarily mean that the conflict is resolved. Rather, it means that the couple chooses the best option for handling a conflict. The couple needs to decide on the way that best protects their interests. There are generally five effective styles of managing conflict: *avoidance, compromise, accommodation, confrontation,* and *collaboration.* The sixth, *competition,* is considered ineffective. The choice of conflict management style hinges on factors such as the conflict's nature, the couple's requirements, and the state of their relationship. In Africa, cultural preferences or expectations may further influence the chosen style. Historically, African cultures have often favored men, affording them greater latitude than women. However, this dynamic is evolving with the increasing recognition of gender rights in many African countries. Notably, these conflict management styles have demonstrated efficacy in cross-cultural contexts as well.

Avoidance: Evading direct discussion of the conflict is seen to be damaging a good relationship. Avoidance is a strategy employed in conflicts when one feels either powerful or powerless. Implementing this approach requires discernment and wisdom from the couple, as there are instances where timing becomes a crucial factor.

Compromise: Giving up something to overcome a stalemate or deadlock (gridlock). Both spouses give up or get something out of the conflict resolution. They do this to reach a quick decision and end the discussion.

Accommodation: Creating a way forward toward a major resolution by giving a pass on mistakes (oversight) either party may have made. In other words, instead of first trying to deal with what was done wrong and by whom, the couple agrees to move on toward a resolution of a bigger issue or to beat a deadline. This style creates peace by minimizing resistance and negativity. However, it should be used sparingly.

Confrontation: Confrontation ignores the feelings of the spouse and sends a message of control. However, when dealing with issues of spouse unfaithfulness, dishonesty, abuse, and addiction, this style is preferred to initiate a conflict resolution. For that reason, confrontation is not necessarily a negative approach. The terms "confrontation" and "conversation" imply an exchange of ideas, sharing a common prefix "con," which stands for "with." Susan Scott asserts that both words essentially carry the same meaning. She emphasizes that confrontation is not about attacking someone from a distance but instead involves sitting side by side and jointly examining the issue."[113] One can imagine what could happen if couples sat side by side talking about the issue that confronts them rather than sitting face to face with the issue between them. One posture suggests the couple facing the issue

---

[113] Susan Scott, Fierce Conversations (New York: New American Library, 2002), p. 152.

objectively, while the other suggests the couple facing each other and discussing the issue subjectively. This is transformative thinking.

Collaboration: Achieving a resolution where both spouses' goals are satisfied is the essence of collaboration. This process demands time, energy, and mutual respect for each other's objectives. Comprehensive consideration is given to various aspects of the conflict, leading the couple to settle on the optimal solution that brings happiness to both parties. Ultimately, it creates a win-win situation.

Competition: Competition usually sends a message that the issue is more important than the relationship. It usually ends in separation or divorce. Consequently, competition isolates itself from other conflict management styles because it is deemed unproductive within a marital relationship. In contrast, the remaining conflict management styles are considered complementary and interdependent, as each represents a viable approach that spouses can employ. Proficiency in communication skills is essential for effectively implementing each of these styles.

Communication Skills in Conflict Management

Effective communication is important in conflict management. Keeping communication lines flowing requires managing (1) emotions, (2) information, and (3) process. We discuss these, respectively.

Managing emotions. When individuals are deeply invested in an issue, emotions can run high, potentially hindering effective conflict management. It is crucial to recognize the signs of becoming overly emotional and, in such instances, call for a time-out to disengage from the interaction. This step helps prevent emotions from spiraling out of control. It is advisable to steer clear of aggressive communication, such as name-calling or personal attacks, as well as other actions that threaten the face of the other person. Additionally, avoiding emotional exaggerations and extremes contributes to a more constructive conflict resolution process. One can be emotional without being belligerent. Describe your emotions and ask your spouse to describe theirs when the situation becomes tense. Sometimes, emotions are part of the conflict and need to be discussed before they lead to volcanic eruptions. Listen and watch yourself in the process. Ask yourself: What emotions am I displaying? How will my spouse respond to those displays? Select a time and place that fosters a relaxed atmosphere for effective interaction. Optimal conditions for discussing conflicts involve avoiding fatigue or being overwhelmed with work, such as at the end of the day. Additionally, refrain from engaging in actions that can be perceived as hurtful or inappropriate during these discussions.

Managing information. When you plan your messaging, it helps to anticipate how the other person might react, so you choose the language that is least likely to evoke a strong emotional reaction. Each spouse should focus on solving the problem and avoid the temptation to focus on evaluating the other. Openness is crucial in maintaining trust; withholding information undermines trust and may prompt a similar response from your spouse. Particularly when couples are under pressure, it is common for them to neglect the importance of taking time to articulate the issue in a more constructive and clear manner.

Managing process. To improve the process of conflict resolution, the couple needs to state clearly what the problem is, agree on the definition of the problem, identify reasons for the problem, articulate the impact of the problem, focus on the problem, state areas of agreement and disagreement; then state a mutually accepted goal or outcome.[114] Employing ultimatums, making demands, using sex as a bargaining tool, revisiting past issues, and refusing to engage in conversation are counterproductive and manipulative tactics. These approaches often hinder healthy communication and resolution in a relationship.

Dealing with the Extended Family

Conflict resolution and management among African families should consider the impact on the extended family. As has been observed earlier, in Africa, marriage is more than the relationship

---

[114] Olsen, DeFrain, and Skogrand, p. 139. See also Carolyn Schrock-Shed, ed., pp. 177-180.

between husband and wife and their nuclear family. Marriage relationships extend beyond the couple to encompass the broader clan or community, incorporating their traditions and identity. Consequently, issues impacting the couple often have a ripple effect, affecting other family members and members of the clan.

To maintain good relationships in the African context requires group communication skills or the knowledge of group dynamics as understood within the African practice. Even if a couple resides in the diaspora, it doesn't sever ties with their extended family. African families maintain connections regardless of distance. Modern technologies, such as the Internet, WhatsApp, Facebook, Twitter, and cell phones, facilitate live discussions involving members of the extended family, even those residing in remote places. Physical contact is also possible with extended family members in the same diasporic geographical area.

Effectively managing conflict involving extended family members requires an understanding of the various communicative roles played by individuals within the group. This understanding is crucial to ensure that the family remains cohesive throughout the conversation. In problem-solving and conflict resolution, the climate is usually tense and emotionally charged. Infante, Rancer and Womack suggest several effective emotional climate roles that can be used in the resolution of conflict when groups are involved.[115] The social and emotional climate in the group can determine the outcome. Sometimes, good ideas and suggestions are lost due to emotional interference. Therefore, creating a conducive emotional climate requires roles, as shown in the diagram below:

---

[115] Dominic A. Infante, Andrew S. Rancer, and Deanna F. Womack, *Building Communication Theory*, 3rd Ed. (Prospect Heights, IL: Waveland Press, 1997), pp. 294-295.

Diagram 6. Good Emotional Climate Roles

The above diagram presents an ideal group setting where each member in the group assumes one or more of these roles to arrive at a resolution. These roles are not assigned, but members, by virtue of their individual skills, unconsciously play these roles. The *encourager* gives positive feedback and warmth; the *harmonizer* mediates to reduce tension; the *compromiser* makes sure each party gains; the *gatekeeper* opens communication channels for everybody to participate; the *standard setter* makes sure evaluation standards are in place; *group communicator* has an interest in the process and group climate; and *follower* simply confirms, conforms, and listens.

Regrettably, in the African extended family system, participants in conflict resolution are often determined by factors such as status, relationship, and age rather than based on their skills in conflict resolution. It is common for individuals in specific family roles or positions to direct the resolution proceedings or conversations. In such situations, the roles of harmonizer and gatekeeper become crucial in managing and navigating these dynamics.

In other words, the group should have its own checks and balances. The number of participants is not as important as the roles that are needed to create a good climate. This implies that certain participants may take on multiple roles. In situations where only spouses are involved, each can adopt any of the mentioned roles to foster a positive climate and achieve a favorable outcome. It's acknowledged that couples often find themselves operating from a defensive-subjective mode, making it challenging to embody the roles mentioned. Assuming an objective pro-solution position, even in the midst of emotional distress, demands significant self-discipline and self-control.

Acquiring skills for conflict resolution is essential for couples, and seeking professional counseling is highly recommended. It's crucial for couples to cultivate a spirit of discernment and insight to recognize their limitations. Seeking professional help promptly, before issues escalate beyond control, is an important step in maintaining a healthy and constructive relationship.

Meaning of Conflict

As communication forms the foundation of human, marital, and family relationships, it's important to view conflict through a communicative lens. Mark V. Redmond, a renowned figure in communication, defines conflict as the interaction between interdependent individuals regarding genuine or perceived conflicting goals or hindrances in achieving those goals.[116] To simplify, conflict arises when people interact and face challenges in pursuing their goals, whether real or perceived.

Conflict involves interaction or conversation. This means that there's no conflict until you directly raise the issue with another person who is deemed responsible for the action, decision, or solution. Interaction implies that two individuals are engaged in a conversation about something meaningful to both parties. This is why conflict is described as a reflection of caring. When couples cease to care about a particular matter or each other, communication breaks down. Therefore, in every conflict, it can be inferred that there is a significant element that the couples are unwilling to forfeit.

---

[116] Mark V. Redmond, Communication: Theories and Application (Boston, NY: Houghton Mifflin Company, 2000), pp. 130-137.

Conflict involves people who are interdependent. This refers to people who are both dependent on each other for the solution, especially when one party is limited in strategies or actions that are needed to resolve the conflict. Yet, genuine conflict doesn't arise when one person is solely dependent on the other; what emerges is merely hostility and frustration, not true conflict. In a marital relationship, as husband and wife are considered equal partners, dependency exists for both in seeking solutions, even if resources are not evenly matched. Conversely, in the parent-child dynamic, you may encounter hostility or frustration rather than conflict because of the inherent power imbalance. However, this dynamic might shift when children grow into adults and parents become dependent.

Conflict involves the parties' goals. There are two types of goals: those that only one party can attain, such as when it is agreed that the wife is going to graduate with a degree before the husband does. This is called an indivisible or inseparable goal. It's the "winner-take-all goal", akin to sports where only one person or team prevails, and "opposing goals," where the objectives of each spouse hinder the other's achievement. The other type is opposing goals. This occurs when one party perceives its goal as obstructed by the goals of the other. Such conflicts often arise in relationships when couples have competing goals or differing visions.

Indeed, this comprehensive understanding of conflict provides a holistic framework for its meaning. Yet, beyond the definition of conflict, it's equally important to consider the aspects and perspectives of those individuals involved in the conflict. According to Turner and West, we must consider (1) the background and personalities of the individuals, (2) goals, rules, emotions, and attributes, (3) strategies, messaging, and communication, (4) immediate results or consequences of a conflict episode, and finally (5) the long-term results of a conflict.[117] In the case of husband and wife, their backgrounds, personalities, emotions, and attributes are a factor in how conflict is resolved. Due to their inherent differences, individuals may not always share the same perspectives, approaches, feelings, or experiences. Hence, it becomes

---

[117] Turner and West, pp. 152-153.

essential to engage in active listening and ask each other questions for clarification when working towards resolving conflicts.

Additionally, it is crucial to cultivate skills related to rules, messaging, and communication strategies. As discussed earlier in this book, understanding the distinct male-female differences in the brain is vital. This understanding aids in comprehending potential challenges stemming from communication differences. Recognizing that marriage involves the union of a man and a woman with inherent differences in chemistry, it becomes apparent that they complement each other. While diverse perspectives may give rise to conflicts, welcoming these differences is essential for fostering constructive conversations.

Every solution that is arrived at has immediate and long-term consequences. These should not be overlooked when the couple is under pressure to get the problem off their shoulders. It's easy to pay attention to desired results and overlook the immediate and long-term consequences. However, it is sometimes possible that the couple may choose to sacrifice the immediate for the sake of the long-term consequences. Couples can navigate these challenges by choosing to face the immediate difficulties together and dealing with the long-term consequences as they arise. Alternatively, they may opt to channel their efforts into preventing immediate consequences and address the long-term ones when they approach that juncture. This approach becomes feasible, particularly when the solution involves a phased strategy.

Conflict management should consider the couple's cultural context and cultural views on conflict. For example, Beebe, Beebe, and Ivy observe that an individualistic culture (Western) operates differently from a collectivistic culture (African).[118] In the case of African families in the diaspora, whose background is collective but living in an individualistic context, this dual experience poses a dilemma in how the couple resolves conflict.

These two cultural contexts frequently clash, underscoring the importance for couples to comprehend the influence each cultural

---

[118]   Beebe, Beebe, and Ivy, p. 222.

setting has on their conflict resolution. In an individualistic cultural context, the emphasis is on prioritizing the individual over the group. In other words, what matters is what the individual feels is important to him or her. Yet the collective cultural context puts the group over the individual. This means that the group is a more dominant player in the process of conflict resolution. African traditions typically lean towards collectivism. To effectively address the challenge posed by this dual experience and navigate conflicts within African families, it becomes crucial to employ various conflict management styles. These styles are outlined below.

Biblical Basis for Resolving Conflicts

Following are Bible verses that are a plausible guide to resolving conflict and show why conflict resolution is important:[119]

- ➢ *Anger management*: "A gentle answer deflects anger, but harsh words make tempers flare." Prov. 15:1

- ➢ *Extending forgiveness*: "Love prospers when a fault is forgiven, but dwelling on it separates close friends." Prov. 17:9

- ➢ *Exercising self-control*: "Starting a quarrel is like opening a floodgate, so stop before a dispute breaks out." Prov. 17:14

- ➢ *Avoiding retaliation*: "Don't say, 'I will get even for this wrong.' Wait for the Lord to handle the matter." Prov. 20:22

- ➢ *Practicing humility*: "Commit yourself to instruction; listen carefully to words of knowledge." Prov. 23:12

- ➢ *Guided by convictions*: "Fire tests the purity of silver and gold, but a person is tested by being praised [flattery]." Prov. 27:21

---

[119] New Living Translation version used in these texts.

➤ *Willingness to confess:* "People who conceal their sins will not prosper, but if they confess and turn from them, they will receive mercy." Prov. 28:13: Matt 5:25

➤ *Real Peacemaker:* "I am leaving you with a gift—peace of mind and heart. And the peace I give is a gift the world cannot give. So don't be troubled or afraid." Jn 14:27

When we talk about resolving conflict, we can learn a lesson from laminin proteins. In biology, laminin proteins play a role in the basement membrane, serving various functions, including holding or binding tissues and organs together. While the biological processes are more intricate, simplifying them for this discussion emphasizes a key point. Credit for this concept goes to Dr. David Mbungu, a biology professor at Andrews University.

To explain the function of laminin, one must think about the skin and why when one grows old, it sags but doesn't drop off from the bones. The skin has three layers: the outside layer (epidermis), composed of epithelial cells; the middle layer (dermis), with connective tissue where you find blood vessels and sweat glands, among others; the third is the fat layer, also called the hypodermis. Indeed, within the layers of the skin, laminins, acting as adhesive basement membranes, play a crucial role between the outer epidermis and the middle dermis. Their function is to bind and hold the dermis and epidermis together, ensuring that even if the skin sags, these layers remain connected. The adhesive properties of laminins serve to maintain the cohesion and integrity of the skin's structure.

As Christians, faith in Jesus Christ should hold couples and families together, as does laminins. As laminins defy the power of gravity that tries to cause the skin to drop off when it sags, so should faith in Jesus Christ defy any challenges that seek to separate family relationships. This is what Colossians 1:17 means: "In Christ, all things hold together."

Similarly, Ellen G. White states: "The cause of division and discord in families and in the church is separation from Christ. To come near to Christ is to come near to one another. The secret of true unity in the church and in the family is not diplomacy, not management, not a superhuman effort to overcome difficulties—though there will be much of this to do—but union with Christ" (*Adventist Home, p. 179*).

The cross-like formation of laminins adds another intriguing dimension, providing an opportunity to draw a spiritual lesson from it. Colossians 1:19-20 says that "through the cross, God has effected a reconciliation of all things to Himself, whether things on earth or things in heaven" (NKJV, paraphrased). Given that laminins possess glue-like properties, are present in every cell in the body, and play a pivotal role in holding cells and tissues together to resist stress and prevent separation, they become a symbolic lesson akin to the cross of Christ imprinted in every cell of our bodies. Understanding laminins extends to implications for how we relate as human beings and how we treat the rest of God's creation.

APPLICATION: What is your understanding of the nature of conflict? Which conflict management style (s) do you use the most? What kind of results do you get?

Chapter 7

INTIMATE VIOLENCE

"When childhood is out of control, adulthood will take control." Ron Rockey

Presently, intimate or domestic violence stands as a significant societal concern, persisting despite heightened awareness and efforts from law enforcement, courts, human and social service organizations, legislators, pastors, and churches. African communities in the diaspora are not an exception to this abusive act that defies common sense logic. The realization is increasingly clear that legislative measures alone cannot transform the human heart. Our endeavor is to persuade individuals in marital and family relationships that a sincere personal commitment to refrain from any manifestation of violence should be regarded with utmost seriousness.

Intimate violence has nothing to do with ethnicity, race, religious affiliation, or even any geographical area. Intimate violence plagues every culture. Therefore, our deliberation here is crucial, as this exploration of the resilience of African families in the diaspora would be incomplete without addressing intimate violence. This discourse specifically focuses on African families in the diaspora to raise awareness. Given the diverse manifestations of intimate violence, it is undeniable that a considerable number of marital and family breakdowns among Africans in the diaspora can be linked to some form of violence.

Meaning of Intimate Violence

According to Barbara Couden, intimate violence is "abuse by someone with whom you have or have had an intimate relationship."[120] While intimate violence typically pertains to human-to-human relationships, it is essential to broaden our perspective to encompass the treatment of animals, such as pets. In Africa, a noticeable culture of insensitivity emerges in the treatment of domesticated animals like oxen and donkeys. It is customary in Africa to employ physical force, such as whipping or hitting, when these animals are engaged in tasks like plowing or pulling a cart.

Too often, stripes and scars on the backs and necks of these animals are the evidence of abuse. The individuals administering the blows often rely on whipping or hitting as their primary method of communication with these animals, even though these creatures can comprehend spoken human language. It has been noted that individuals who engage in the mistreatment of pets, animals, and property may also harbor the potential to inflict harm on other people within their intimate relationships.

Intimate (domestic) violent acts encompass a broad spectrum of behaviors, ranging from physical violence such as battering, slapping, shoving, and punching, among other actions. Perpetrators often resort to these physical acts as a substitute for effective communication. In numerous instances, the use of physical violence can be interpreted as a manifestation of weakness, reflecting an inability to articulate thoughts convincingly. Following are different aspects of intimate violence:

> Coercive behavior such as intimidation, threats, and ultimatums. This occurs when an individual utilizes their power to coerce or compel the other person to cooperate or comply, even against their will. This dynamic extends to

---

[120] Barbara Couden, ed. *Understand Intimate Violence* (Hagerstown, MD: Review and Herald Publishing Association, 1999), p. 29.

parent-child relationships, especially in situations where open communication and the freedom to express oneself are lacking.

➤ Psychological (mental or emotional) abuse such as sleep deprivation, sexual assault, ignoring a person, isolating a person from meaningful events, or blocking a person from reporting; passive aggressiveness such as making negative expressions, resentment, sabotage, and non-compliance. Sabotage is the intentional act of sharing information too late, often after damage has occurred or actively obstructing a person from achieving their goals.

➤ Economic dependency is when an abused person stays in an abusive relationship because he/she has no options. A wife enduring abuse may opt to remain with an abusive husband due to factors such as unemployment, financial debt, or an inability to single-handedly care for the children. Economic dependency becomes a coercive tool, holding the victim hostage by conveying that nothing will change unless the abuser's demands are fulfilled. This form of dependency has the detrimental effect of stifling initiative and eroding hope in the abused individual.

➤ The destruction of property constitutes a form of abuse, such as when one kicks a glass door out of anger towards their spouse or intentionally damages a phone to prevent them from reaching out to report an instance of abuse.

➤ Verbal abuse is exhibited through yelling, angry outbursts, name-calling, and frequent accusations. These behaviors often result in emotional damage, such as low self-esteem, trauma, or depression.

➤ A deficiency in adequate parenting skills can manifest as a form of abuse, as seen in instances where a child is told they are unintelligent or not as smart as another child, directly undermining the child's self-esteem. Additionally, unrealistic expectations rooted in a lack of understanding of children's developmental stages may involve treating a child as an adult or expecting a teenager to behave like a junior. This form of abuse encompasses actions such as belittling, screaming, threatening, blaming, and providing inadequate care in terms of food, clothing, shelter, medical attention, or supervision, collectively creating a hostile environment for the child.

Intimate violence can easily occur if we are not consistently vigilant due to its diverse nature. The widespread occurrence of this type of violence has unfortunately led some to perceive it as acceptable behavior, fostering a culture that tolerates violence. Similar to conflict management, addressing intimate violence without considering the cultural context may prove ineffective. When the cultural context is taken into account, it becomes easier to distinguish between abusive behavior and actions that align with cultural norms. Whatever the situation, the person abused must feel abused.

Unfortunately, in some cultural contexts, acts of domestic violence are entrenched in marital relationships and parenting styles. There exists a myth that suggests African women view physical violence as a demonstration of love, considering it an acceptable means of building relationships. However, this perception is a fallacy. Women who seem to accept such treatment may feel compelled to do so because they perceive it as a choice between enduring physical abuse and facing neglect, both of which are forms of mistreatment. In the realm of parenting, there is a belief that corporal punishment is essential for disciplining children. Nevertheless, it's important to acknowledge that while physical punishment may enforce compliance and conformity, it does not lead to genuine transformation and positive behavioral change in the child. The following texts in the Bible are sometimes used to justify spanking children.

> ➤ "My son, do not despise the chastening of the Lord, Nor detest His correction; For whom the Lord loves He corrects, Just as a father, the son *in whom* he delights" Prov. 3:11-12 (NKJV).

> ➤ "He who spares his rod hates his son, But he who loves him disciplines him promptly" Prov. 13:24 (NKJV)

> ➤ "Foolishness *is* bound up in the heart of a child; The rod of correction will drive it far from him" Prov. 22:15 (NKJV).

> ➤ "Do not withhold correction from a child, For *if* you beat him with a rod, he will not die. You shall beat him with a rod, And deliver his soul from hell" Prov. 23:13-14 (NKJV).

> ➤ "The rod and rebuke give wisdom, But a child left to himself brings shame to his mother" Prov. 29:15 (NKJV).

The disciplinary challenge is the matter of physical punishment, such as beating. The correction or discipline of a child should be guided by love, akin to anesthesia, ensuring that any temporary discomfort is administered with care and in moderation. Temporary discomfort, when applied with love, can be seen as a constructive aspect of discipline. Keil and Delitzsch state: "A father who truly wishes well to his son keeps him betimes under strict discipline, to give him while he is yet capable of being influenced the right direction, and to allow no errors to root themselves in him; but he who is indulgent toward his child when he ought to be strict, acts as if he really wished his ruin."[121] Bible texts like Proverbs 13:24 also suggest that the discipline from the Lord shows that He loves us, in the same way, the father's discipline of his son is a sign that he loves him. There are other texts that suggest that God allows (or uses) suffering, adversity, or crises to lead us toward repentance (Deut. 8:5; Job 5:17-27; 33:15-30; Heb. 12:5-6).

---

[121] C. F. Keil and F. Delitzsch, *Commentary on the Old Testament, Proverbs, Ecclesiastes, and Song of Solomon*, Vol. 6 (Peabody, MA: Hendrickson Publishers, Inc., 2006), p. 208.

The above texts need to be understood against the backdrop of the times because "corporal punishment for unruly children was simply taken for granted in ancient Israel and Egypt."[122] The online edition of Word Commentary quotes Van Leeuwen, who states that "when legitimate authority fails to punish, we treat wrongdoers as less than human." In other words, if discipline is withheld from a child, that becomes a recipe for future wrongdoing for which the child may end up incarcerated.

It is crucial to emphasize that the preceding statements do not serve as an endorsement for physically harming or spanking children as a form of parental discipline in contemporary times. Instead, within the context of today's understanding of abuse, these statements advocate for parents to responsibly guide their children through teaching, training, nurturing, and early character development. Correction should be approached conscientiously, prioritizing methods that contribute to the child's growth and well-being. Ellen G. White states: "Children are sometimes tempted to chafe under restraint, but in the afterlife, they will bless their parents for the faithful care and strict watchfulness that guarded and guided them in their years of inexperience."[123] Parents should not be afraid of correcting children for fear of alienation and creating resentment. It should be remembered that "wisdom and common sense are not transferred by being just a good example."[124]

Today, statutory laws are meant to identify acts of violence and punish the perpetrators of acts of violence. According to the Biblical and Christian view (Gen. 1:26-28), every human being is created in the image of God, and therefore, any attempt to control the will of another, including children, is an attack on their image and a violation of that person's identity and dignity. God Himself does not control human will. He says, "Come now, let us reason together" (Isa. 1:18). The

---

[122] *Word Biblical Commentary*, WordSearch online, accessed April 22, 2019.

[123] Ellen G. White, *The Ministry of Healing* (Silver Spring, MD: Better Living Publications, 1990), p. 165.

[124] Footnote on Proverbs 22:15, in *Life Application Study Bible* (Grand Rapids, MI: Zondervan, 2007), p. 1342.

contrast is clear: God talks, man forces. An abuser assumes a role that even the Creator of the universe does not assume. E. G. White states: "The inhumanity of man toward man is our greatest sin. Many think that they are representing the justice of God while they wholly fail to represent His tenderness and His great love."[125]

To manage conflict and improve parenting skills, spouses need to evidence the character of Jesus Christ in daily life according to the Scriptures below:

➤ Eph. 4:22-24: *"That you put off, concerning your former conduct, the old man which grows corrupt according to the deceitful lusts, and be renewed in the spirit of your mind, and that you put on the new man which was created according to God, in true righteousness and holiness."*

➤ Deut. 6:1-4: *"Now this is the commandment, and these are the statutes and judgments which the Lord your God has commanded to teach you, that you may observe them in the land which you are crossing over to possess, ²that you may fear the Lord your God, to keep all His statutes and His commandments which I command you, you and your son and your grandson, all the days of your life, and that your days may be prolonged. ³Therefore hear, O Israel, and be careful to observe it, that it may be well with you, and that you may multiply greatly as the Lord God of your fathers has promised you—'a land flowing with milk and honey.' ⁴"Hear, O Israel: The Lord our God, the Lord is one! ⁵You shall love the Lord your God with all your heart, with all your soul, and with all your strength."*

➤ 1Cor. 13:1-8, 13: *"Though I speak with the tongues of men and of angels, but have not love, I have become sounding brass or a clanging cymbal. ²And though I have the gift of prophecy, and understand all mysteries and all knowledge, and though I have all faith, so that I could remove mountains, but have not love, I am nothing. ³And*

---

[125] Ellen G. White, *Ministry of Healing* (Mountain View, CA: Pacific Press Publishing Association, 1942), p. 163.

though I bestow all my goods to feed the poor, and though I give my body to be burned, but have not love, it profits me nothing. ⁴Love suffers long and is kind; love does not envy; love does not parade itself, is not puffed up; ⁵does not behave rudely, does not seek its own, is not provoked, thinks no evil; ⁶does not rejoice in iniquity, but rejoices in the truth; ⁷bears all things, believes all things, hopes all things, endures all things. ⁸Love never fails . . . And now abide faith, hope, love, these three; but the greatest of these is love."

> Eph.5:17-29: "Therefore do not be unwise, but understand what the will of the Lord is. ¹⁸And do not be drunk with wine, in which is dissipation; but be filled with the Spirit, ¹⁹speaking to one another in psalms and hymns and spiritual songs, singing and making melody in your heart to the Lord, ²⁰giving thanks always for all things to God the Father in the name of our Lord Jesus Christ, ²¹submitting to one another in the fear of God. ²²Wives, submit to your own husbands, as to the Lord. ²³For the husband is head of the wife, as also Christ is head of the church; and He is the Savior of the body. ²⁴Therefore, just as the church is subject to Christ, so let the wives be to their own husbands in everything. ²⁵Husbands, love your wives, just as Christ also loved the church and gave Himself for her, ²⁶that He might sanctify and cleanse her with the washing of water by the word, ²⁷that He might present her to Himself a glorious church, not having spot or wrinkle or any such thing, but that she should be holy and without blemish. ²⁸So husbands ought to love their own wives as their own bodies; he who loves his wife loves himself. ²⁹For no one ever hated his own flesh, but nourishes and cherishes it, just as the Lord does the church."

The passage in Ephesians 5:21-33, often cited with the instruction for wives to submit to their husbands, is indeed one that has been subject to various interpretations. George R. Knight sheds light on this text by considering the historical context of Greek-Roman times. In those times, the term "submit" was commonly used in a military context, implying that a subordinate should yield to a superior.

However, Paul's use of the term within this biblical passage differs. Instead of emphasizing a hierarchical authority, Paul frames it within the context of a love relationship, where the husband's role is characterized by responsibility rather than mere positional authority. In this interpretation, the concept of submission is not rooted in the wife's inferiority but is rather an expression of equality. The wife's submission is seen as reflective of her role within the context of the equal worth of both partners in the relationship.

Paul likened the husband as the head of the wife to Christ as the Head of the church (His bride). Because Christ loved the church so much that He gave Himself up for her, the husband should also act sacrificially and lovingly toward his wife. He should render care rather than control.[126] Paul uses the same understanding of submission when talking about children and slaves in relationship to parents and masters, respectively. His message to Christian believers rises above cultural norms to treat people "in the atmosphere of the Lord."[127]

What to Do About Abuse

Addressing abuse is undoubtedly a complex and challenging task. Acknowledging that there may be no enduring human solution to the complexities of the human condition is an insightful perspective. The Bible is often considered a guide in articulating the human condition, serving as a mirror that reflects one's own circumstances rather than someone else's. This recognition underscores the importance of humility and self-reflection in approaching the complexities of human relationships and conditions.

In Romans 3:9-18 Paul boldly describes the human condition as follows:

> What shall we conclude then? Do we have any advantage? Not at all! For we have already made the charge that Jews and Gentiles alike are all under the power of sin. [10]As it is written: There is no one righteous, not even one; [11]there is no one who

---

126 Ibid., p. 280.
127 Ibid., p. 282.

understands; there is no one who seeks God. [12]All have turned away, they have together become worthless; there is no one who does good, not even one. [13]Their throats are open graves; their tongues practice deceit. The poison of vipers is on their lips. [14]Their mouths are full of cursing and bitterness. [15]Their feet are swift to shed blood; [16]ruin and misery mark their ways, [17]and the way of peace they do not know. [18] There is no fear of God before their eyes (NKJV).

Considering this graphic description of the human condition, elsewhere Paul sends a warning: *"Therefore let him who thinks he stands take heed lest he fall"* (1Cor 10:12, NKJV). Facing the reality that humanity is flawed, marked by a tendency to communicate and act in ways that fall short of glorifying God and uplifting one another, is an important acknowledgment. The term "edify," meaning to improve through teaching and instruction, underscores the human need for positive guidance. Human beings often exhibit destructive tendencies, neglecting to build and nurture each other. Intimate violence can be seen as a manifestation of this inherent human condition. It becomes imperative for individuals to seek ways to transcend these shortcomings and enhance their relationships.

Following the example set by Jesus Christ is presented as a path toward achieving this improvement. Emulating Christ's teachings and actions can provide a foundation for positive change, fostering healthier and more constructive relationships among individuals.

This takes us back to our previous discussion about the need to align our beliefs and behaviors. Those who profess to be followers of Jesus need to act like Jesus. We are told that "Jesus grew in wisdom and in stature and in favor with God and all the people" (Luke 2:52, NLT). This means Jesus developed mentally, physically, spiritually, and socially. We, too, are called to exhibit the same: *"'You must love the LORD your God with all your heart, all your soul, and all your mind.' This is the first and greatest commandment. A second is equally important: 'Love your neighbor as yourself.' The entire law and all the demands of the prophets are based on these two commandments."*

Certainly, examining Jesus' conduct in His human relationships reveals a genuine example of growing in favor with both God and humankind. Notably, Jesus demonstrated a unique and compassionate approach in his interactions with women. In the story found in John 4, where Jesus encounters a sinful woman at the well, his conversation stands out as distinctive from what she might have experienced with other men. In this interaction, Jesus looked beyond the woman's current circumstances, recognizing her potential to become a dignified daughter of God rather than someone to be exploited or condemned. This portrayal emphasizes Jesus' ability to see the intrinsic value and transformative potential in every individual.

The Gospels depict Jesus as a compassionate and understanding individual, displaying genuine care and respect in his interactions with women. In Luke 7:36-50, when a sinful woman publicly anointed Jesus, he did not recoil or take offense. Instead, he graciously accepted both the gesture and the woman, recognizing her potential as a daughter of God.

Another significant example is found in Jesus' relationship with Mary and Martha, the sisters of Lazarus. Despite the societal norms of his time, Jesus demonstrated the ability to be a true friend to women, maintaining respectful and meaningful conversations with them. His choice to spend time in Bethany, where Mary and Martha lived, reflects his genuine connection and care for these women.

In Mark 5, the account of the woman with a twelve-year-long issue of bleeding highlights Jesus' transformative impact. Despite societal norms that may have marginalized her, Jesus recognized her as somebody, affirming her worth and upgrading her status through their encounter. This pattern of treating women with dignity and recognizing their intrinsic value is a consistent theme in Jesus' interactions throughout the Gospels.

Jesus upgraded children as well. In Luke 18:16, we read: *"Then Jesus called for the children and said to the disciples, 'Let the children come to me. Don't stop them! For the Kingdom of God belongs to those who are like these children'"* (NLT). Indeed, Jesus demonstrated a profound care and value for children, emphasizing their importance and treating them with dignity. His welcoming attitude, such as allowing children to sit on his lap, conveyed a sense of safety and affirmation of their worth. In contrast to this positive perspective on children, today's reality often involves risks for children both within their homes and in public spaces.

Unfortunately, the threat to children's well-being can come from various sources, including family members. It is a sobering realization that dangers to children can exist within their immediate environment, not just from strangers. This underscores the importance of creating safe and nurturing environments for children, raising awareness about potential risks, and working collectively to protect and prioritize the well-being of the younger members of society.

The safety of children is strictly in the hands of parents and guardians. Parents need information to increase their knowledge of childrearing skills. It is, unfortunately, true that many families only realize the severity of abuse after its damaging effects have become apparent. Disturbingly, Christians are not immune to engaging in abusive behaviors. In Matthew 5:14-16, followers of Jesus are described as "the light of the world," and their Christian behavior is meant to serve as a witness to those around them. Despite knowing what is right, parents, like anyone else, may sometimes act differently.

As Christians, there should be a concerted effort to prevent intimate violence and abuse. Striving to embody the teachings of compassion, love, and respect that are central to Christian principles can contribute to fostering healthier relationships and preventing the cycle of abuse. The acknowledgment of the issue within Christian communities is a crucial step toward promoting awareness, education, and, ultimately, positive change. Jesus said, *"Not so with you. Instead, whoever wants to become great among you must be your servant, and whoever wants to be first must be your slave – just as the Son of Man did not come to be served, but to serve, and to give his life as a ransom for many"* (Matt. 20:26-28 NIV).

Jesus knew how to communicate without being abusive. In Matthew 12:18-21, we read about how Isaiah, in his prophecy, described Jesus:

"Here is my servant whom I have chosen, the one I love, in whom I delight; I will put my Spirit on him, and he will proclaim justice to the nations. He will not quarrel or cry out; no one will hear his voice in the streets. A bruised reed he will not break, and a smoldering wick he will not snuff out, till he has brought justice through to victory. In his name the nations will put their hope."

Certainly, the portrayal of Jesus in the Bible reflects a multifaceted character. While He is recognized as a King, He exhibits justice with tenderness and gentleness, especially toward those who are weak, powerless, and marginalized. His interactions with such individuals emphasize compassion, understanding, and an inclination to uplift rather than exacerbate their conditions.

The "Woe" utterances in Matthew 23, directed at the Scribes and Pharisees, are often cited to demonstrate Jesus' strong words. However, these utterances can be understood as an expression of Jesus speaking truth to power, particularly when addressing situations where the poor and marginalized were being exploited. In these instances, Jesus did not shy away from confronting injustice and abusive behavior. His words were meant to challenge and rectify, emphasizing the importance of addressing wrongdoing rather than condoning it through silence or smooth talk. Ellen G. White described Jesus as a communicator:

> In His intercourse with others, He exercised the greatest tact, and He was always kind and thoughtful. He was never rude, never needlessly spoke a severe word, and never gave unnecessary pain to a sensitive soul. He did not censure human weakness. He fearlessly denounced hypocrisy, unbelief, and iniquity, but tears were in His voice as He uttered His scathing rebukes. He never made truth cruel but never manifested a deep tenderness for humanity. Every soul was precious in His sight. He bore Himself with divine dignity, yet He bowed with the tenderest compassion and regard to

every member of the family of God. He saw in all souls whom it was His mission to save."[128]

The attributes demonstrated by Christ, such as justice, tenderness, gentleness, compassion, and truth-telling, should indeed be reflected in our marital, familial, and interpersonal relationships. The transformative power of the gospel should permeate all aspects of our lives, leading to a profound change in character.

The concept of transformation, as explained by Evan B. Howard in "The Brazos Introduction to Christian Spirituality," involves a shift from one form to another and a change in relationship that results in a reorientation of life towards God. This God-ward reorientation is a process that, in turn, gives rise to character transformation. It emphasizes the interconnectedness of faith and action, as faith without corresponding works is considered inactive, as noted in James 2:17. True transformation encompasses a holistic change that extends to our thoughts, actions, and relationships, aligning them with the principles of love, justice, and compassion exemplified by Christ.

According to Howard, transformation means repentance (2 Tim. 1:9), which is a change of attitude. Transformation also means conversion, which covers broad aspects that include growing relationally with God, growing mentally in our beliefs, growing morally in our values and lifestyle, growing religiously in our sense of identity, growing socially in our relationships, and growing ecologically in our relationship with the rest of God's creation.[129]

The Christian faith presents a holistic view of life, and when taken seriously and practiced, intimate violence will have no place among Christians and in society. In Romans 12:1-2 we read: *"And so, dear brothers and sisters, I plead with you to give your bodies to God because of all he has done for you. Let them be a living and holy sacrifice—the kind he will find acceptable. This is truly the way to worship him. Don't copy the behavior and customs of this world, but let God transform you into a new person by*

---

[128] Ellen G. White, *Gospel Workers* (Washington, D.C.: Review and Herald Publishing Association, 1915), p. 117.
[129] Ibid., pp. 255-258.

changing the way you think. Then you will learn to know God's will for you,
which is good and pleasing and perfect."

The idea of Christians as "being saved" in 1 Corinthians 1:18 suggests an ongoing and dynamic experience rather than a one-time event. This aligns with the broader Biblical perspective that emphasizes a continual unfolding of understanding and knowledge as an individual's journey through life.

The concept of progressive revelation is fundamental in this understanding, highlighting that as we experience different phases in life and encounter various aspects of God and ourselves, our knowledge deepens. This progression underscores the idea that religious experiences should not be superficial but rather possess depth, with believers continually seeking to grow in their understanding of God and align their lives with the transformative teachings of Christianity. Ellen G. White shares a similar view on Christian living when she says:

> The home should be a place where cheerfulness, courtesy, and love abide, and where these graces dwell, there will abide happiness and peace. Troubles may invade, but these are the lot of humanity. Let patience, gratitude, and love keep sunshine in the heart, though the day may be ever so cloudy. In such homes, angels of God abide. Let the husband and wife study each other's happiness, never failing in the small courtesies, and little kindly acts that cheer and brighten the life.[130]

Christian character transformation

It's clear that Christian character transformation plays a pivotal role in intimate and interpersonal relationships, particularly within the family unit. When individuals fail to align their lives with the teachings of Christ, it can lead to dysfunction in marital and family dynamics. The concept of sanctification, often described as the work

---

[130]   Ellen G. White, *Ministry of Healing* (Silver Spring, MD: Better Living Publications, 1990), p. 165.

of a lifetime, can be challenging to articulate. The attempt to illustrate sanctification as a journey with Jesus Christ through five levels is a helpful framework. The use of prepositions (without, to, of, in, with) to distinguish these levels provides a tangible way to explain the different stages of this transformative journey with Christ. This framework can serve as a guide for individuals seeking to understand and navigate the process of aligning their lives with Christ and growing in sanctification.

Here are two diagrams (labeled 7 and 8) depicting the progression of one's relationship with Christ. Diagram 7 provides a visual representation of the growth process in Christ, highlighting that this journey is not consistently linear or always ascending. Rather, it illustrates fluctuations with both upward and downward phases. There are periods of active growth and moments of slowdown. The diagram aims to convey that even during downturns, the low points should surpass the previous ones, emphasizing that although progress is made in the relationship with Jesus, there are instances of temporary dysfunction.

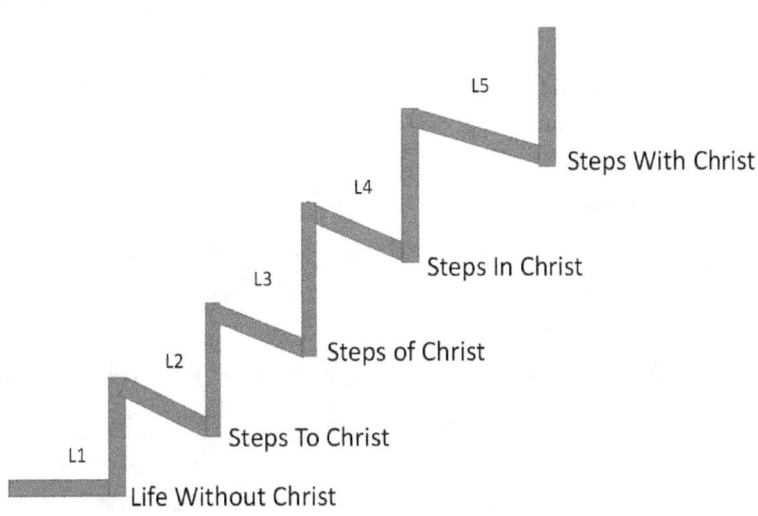

Diagram 7: What growing in Christ looks like

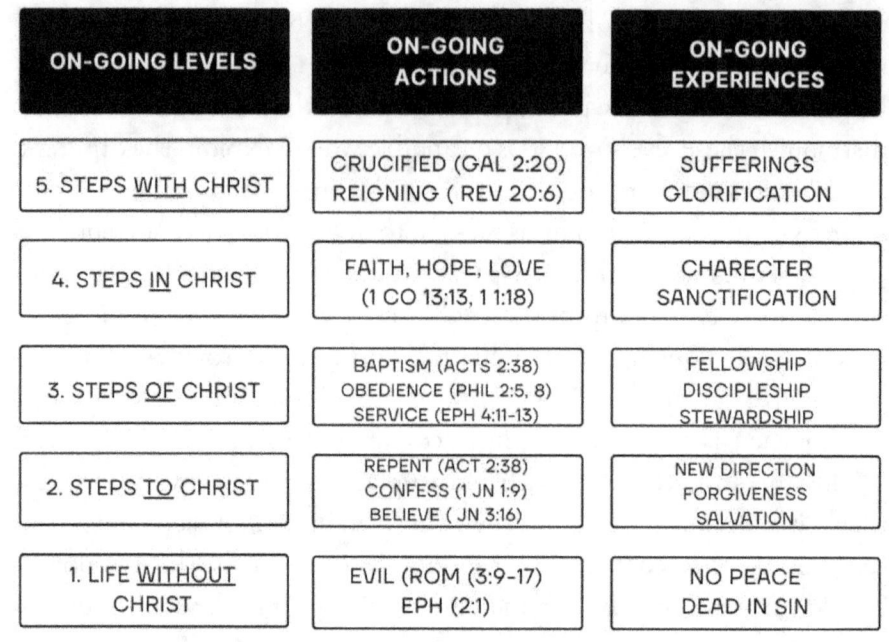

ON-GOING LEVELS	ON-GOING ACTIONS	ON-GOING EXPERIENCES
5. STEPS WITH CHRIST	CRUCIFIED (GAL 2:20) REIGNING (REV 20:6)	SUFFERINGS GLORIFICATION
4. STEPS IN CHRIST	FAITH, HOPE, LOVE (1 CO 13:13, 1 1:18)	CHARECTER SANCTIFICATION
3. STEPS OF CHRIST	BAPTISM (ACTS 2:38) OBEDIENCE (PHIL 2:5, 8) SERVICE (EPH 4:11-13)	FELLOWSHIP DISCIPLESHIP STEWARDSHIP
2. STEPS TO CHRIST	REPENT (ACT 2:38) CONFESS (1 JN 1:9) BELIEVE (JN 3:16)	NEW DIRECTION FORGIVENESS SALVATION
1. LIFE WITHOUT CHRIST	EVIL (ROM (3:9-17) EPH (2:1)	NO PEACE DEAD IN SIN

Diagram 8. Meaning of Growing in Christ

Diagram 8 indicates that the journey with Jesus Christ commences from a starting point, characterized by a lack of knowledge about Jesus (Rom. 3:17), actions conflicting with God's purposes, and inner restlessness. Progressing to Level 2 requires the steps of accepting Jesus Christ, repenting, confessing, and believing. The central part of the chart outlines the experiences necessary to advance to levels 3, 4, and 5, with Level 5 representing the ultimate and final stage anticipated to occur at the Second Coming of Christ. It is possible that a Christian experience can fall back or lapse. For this reason, it is imperative to have a continued dependence on Jesus, "who is able to keep you from stumbling and to present you before his glorious presence without fault and with great joy" (Jude 24). The Application Study Bible's commentary on this verse says: "To be sinless and perfect. . . will be the ultimate condition of the believer when he or she finally sees Christ face to face."[131] Ellen G. White is equally clear when she says:

---

[131] Footnote, *Application Study Bible*, NIV edition (Grand Rapids, MI: Zondervan, 2005), p. 2793.

"When the conflict of life is ended when the armor is laid off at the feet of Jesus when the saints of God are glorified, then and then only will it be safe to claim that we are saved, and sinless."[132] Addressing abuse or intimate violence requires a profound transformation of the human condition and the adoption of a Biblical perspective on life. This involves not only recognizing and rectifying individual behaviors but also cultivating a broader societal understanding that aligns with the principles of compassion, justice, and respect emphasized in the Bible. The process of transformation encompasses a shift in attitudes, values, and interpersonal dynamics, fostering an environment where abuse is not tolerated and individuals are treated with dignity and love.

APPLICATION: What makes intimate violence insidious? How does communicating one's boundaries help prevent intimate violence? Intimate violence goes against God's creation. How?

---

[132] Ellen G. White, *Selected Messages*, Book 3 (Washington, D.C.: Review and Herald Publishing Association, 1980), pp. 355-356.

Chapter 8

THE ATTITUDE OF FORGIVENESS

"There is no future without forgiveness." Desmond Tutu

In the context of content and thriving relationships, embracing a forgiving mindset becomes effortlessly attainable. J. C. Deridder characterizes attitude as reaction "in a definite, meaningful manner towards an object which, on account of the individual's previous experience with it, has an emotional value."[133] This implies that attitude is intricately connected to one's prior experiences with an object, shaping a response that can be either positive or negative.

Given that conflicts are prevalent in marital and family relationships, it can be deduced that forgiveness is an indispensable component for the survival of any marriage. The capacity to forgive is a key factor that sustains relationships, and it is fundamentally driven by love. Consequently, it can be asserted that without love, there is no room for forgiveness, and without forgiveness, the foundation for a successful marriage is compromised. The inclination to forgive is not inherently present in most individuals, as evidenced by common excuses such as "It's too painful for me" or "I cannot forgive unless he/she seeks forgiveness."

One of the biggest excuses people make is, "It's easier said than done." Frequently, such statements serve as an acknowledgment of the

---

[133] J. C. Deridder, *The Personality of the Urban African in South Africa* (London: Routledge & Kegan Paul, 1961), p. 169.

140

necessity for forgiveness coupled with a hesitancy to compromise one's ego. That's how the disciples felt too: "Lord, how many times shall I forgive my brother or sister who sins against me" (Matt. 18:21 NIV)? How do we deal with this kind of thinking? According to Everett L. Worthington Jr., we experience wounds from all kinds of close relationships. Society forces us to make the justice system our default when we wrong one another. The Bible, however, instructs us to turn our wrongs over to God, who cares for us (1 Pet 5:7).[134]

Regrettably, holding onto unforgiveness inflicts harm on both the wrongdoer and the aggrieved party. Unforgiveness has detrimental effects on health, diminishing immune system function and impeding the body's capacity to combat infections. An analogy underscores this impact, suggesting that if a patient harbors anger toward the individual responsible for a fire that caused skin burns, the injured skin may resist the healing process.

Those who study the brain inform us that the thalamus and the hippocampus are part of the limbic system that is responsible for emotional behavior, motivation, and regulation of memories, among other things. In essence, the thalamus functions as an editor for information received from sensory nerves (such as sound, sight, touch, taste, and smell), refining and distributing this information to different areas of the brain. Conversely, the hippocampus plays a role in processing emotional responses and converting information into long-term memory.

As an illustration, Alzheimer's disease is noted for impacting the hippocampus region of the brain. In practical terms, delayed forgiveness allows negative emotions to intensify, evolving into persistent feelings of anger and resentment. Consequently, these emotions find a place in the long-term memory storage of the brain. This underscores the urgency for prompt resolutions, as the presence of unforgiveness subjects the individual to a range of detrimental effects, including anger, pain, hatred, the persistence of negative memories, a desire for revenge, and

---

[134] Everett L. Worthington Jr., *A Just Forgiveness* (Downers Grove, IL: IVP, 2009), p 11.

even difficulty with sleep (insomnia).[135] Forgiveness, on the other hand, offers many benefits, as Jones and Jones state:

> Forgiveness is not just an opportunity but an invitation to redeem failure. Forgiveness is a healing bridge across troubled relationship waters. Forgiveness has as its aims reconciliation and restoration to oneness. Forgiveness sets us free from past ghosts and enables us to interact authentically. Forgiveness clears the passageway to receive mercy from God. Forgiveness paves the road to spiritual growth and overall health. Because of its benefits, forgiveness should be a high-priority item. It is a wide door of hope for the black family.[136]

The statement by Jones and Jones gains particular significance when considering its context, as it addresses the black family in America, which has a history marked by forced migration and ongoing challenges related to slavery. In this specific historical and cultural context, the authors emphasize the importance of forgiveness. Africans, too, can resonate with this historical narrative, drawing parallels to their experiences with colonialism. Given the profound and traumatic history, forgiveness is not merely a choice but a vital necessity. This imperative to forgive extends beyond historical contexts and holds relevance in the realm of marriage as well. To fully appreciate the importance of forgiveness, we must keep the following benefits in mind:[137]

➤ Forgiveness repairs relationships ruptured by sin.

➤ Forgiveness does not eliminate the consequences of sin.

---

[135] Alfred R. Jones and Doris E. Jones, *A Door of Hope for the Black Family* (Pine Forge, PA: Family Outreach Publications, 1998), pp. 24-30.

[136] Ibid., p. 23.

[137] H. D. McDonald, *Forgiveness and Atonement* (Grand Rapids, MI: Baker, 1984), pp. 11-32.

➢ Forgiveness is a gift from God (Neh. 9:17; Mic. 7:18; Gen. 3:15; Exo. 34:6-7; Psa. 32; Psa. 130).

➢ Forgiveness means one side repents and the other forgives.[138]

➢ Forgiveness means the perpetrator asks for it, and the victim grants it.

➢ Forgiveness redeems the past, establishes fellowship, and frees the future.

➢ Forgiveness sets the perpetrator free of guilt and the victim free of pain.

Human Approaches to Guilt

There are three ways by which people deal with guilt and the guilty, particularly in family matters.[139]

Trivialization occurs when guilt is regarded as a mere error or mistake, with the expectation of quick forgiveness due to the belief that human errors are inevitable. This perspective is often taken by spouses who trust that their love can overcome such mistakes. However, if this attitude persists and repetitive errors are not addressed, it can escalate into animosity, leading to a dysfunctional relationship. It is essential for spouses not to take each other for granted and actively collaborate to overcome habitual mistakes.

Retaliation. Responding to guilt with a sense of revenge is a common reaction within families. Lingering negative feelings can escalate into a desire for retribution or vendetta, creating a "gotcha you" moment. This occurs when the guilt of one party is taken seriously, leading the offended individual to believe that the offender must suffer equally to achieve balance. In extreme cases, the offended might take matters into

---

[138] Geiko Muller-Fahrenholz, *The Art of Forgiveness* (Geneva: WCC Publications, 1997), pp. 4-26.
[139] Ibid., pp. 17-22.

their own hands, seeking retaliation. This can become an act of despair when the offended feels there are no alternative paths to healing.

Unforgiveness often manifests prominently in the bedroom, where one spouse may manipulate the other by withholding intimacy until compliance or confession is achieved. This coercive tactic, known as extortion, can strain the marital relationship to the point of divorce. Retaliation may also arise in situations where one spouse justifies an extramarital affair in response to the infidelity of the other, leading to a cycle of blame, often referred to as "tit for tat" among Africans.

These diverse approaches underscore the complexity of dealing with guilt and forgiveness within the intricate dynamics of family relationships.

Courts of justice. Where cases of abuse and violence occur, forgiveness will not prevent the law from taking its course. In such situations, it's crucial for spouses to recognize that expressions of love and forgiveness may not deter the offended party from reporting the issue to law enforcement or social workers. It becomes their responsibility to actively engage in resolving these matters and preventing future occurrences. Reporting instances of abuse, for instance, serves the important purpose of initiating a fair legal process to address the case.

However, it's essential to note that while the punishment of the perpetrator through legal channels may provide a sense of closure for some, it doesn't inherently address the healing process for the victim. The legal resolution serves its purpose of ensuring accountability and justice, but additional measures, such as counseling or support services, may be necessary to aid in the emotional recovery of the victim. This dual approach, involving both legal recourse and support for the victim, can contribute to a more comprehensive and effective resolution of such challenging situations. Forgiveness is an important element that does what the courts of law cannot do; that is, heal our brokenness.

Process of Self-forgiveness

Frequently, the well-being of a marital relationship is compromised by unresolved past events, leading to adverse effects due to the absence of closure and unhealed emotional wounds. Often, a spouse may remain unaware of the lingering impact of old wounds on the marriage until it is brought to light, potentially by a counselor. Instances of denial can exacerbate the situation. Genuine happiness remains elusive until these historical wounds are identified, addressed, and treated. Presented below are seven self-guided steps aimed at uncovering and addressing any lingering issues that might be affecting the marital relationship.

Face it. Acknowledge that there is a problem and determine its root cause. Sometimes, this simple acknowledgment is the first step toward finding a solution. The course of action to resolve the problem may differ based on its nature. It might entail seeking immediate medical attention or counseling. Denying the issue only exacerbates the situation. Ford Rowan emphasizes that self-forgiveness involves acknowledging wrongs committed against others and accepting the repercussions of one's actions. It necessitates the mental challenge of simultaneously occupying the roles of both the wrongdoer and the forgiver.[140]

Forgiving a perpetrator is not that easy to do. A good example is that of Kizita Kalima, a Rwandan genocide survivor, who told his graphic experience to a crowd at the University of Notre Dame, USA, on April 27, 2019. He was a 15-year-old boy when the genocide took place. Enduring various harrowing experiences, he endured a machete wound to the head. Departing his home country, he sought refuge in Tanzania, where he turned to playing basketball to alleviate the posttraumatic stress disorder (PTSD) and depression haunting him. Despite achieving basketball stardom and gaining recognition in the national newspaper, the darkness of depression persisted, leading him to contemplate suicide at times. Eventually relocating to Indiana in

---

[140] Ford Rowan, "Forgiveness and Healing in Prison," Interpretation: A Journal of Bible and Theology, Vol. 72, No. 3 (July 2018), p. 298.

the United States, he underwent medical treatment, yet his condition remained unchanged. In a poignant revelation, he confessed, "I chose to forgive that I might live." Confronting his challenges directly ushered in a transformative change in his life.

Confronting one's experience of suffering requires the following steps:

Trace it. This means doing what doctors do before they administer treatment. They try to find out what the problem is, when it happened, who caused it, why it happened that way, and what may have caused that person to act the way he/she did. By tracing it, the aim is to get to the root of the problem.

Tell it. Share your story. Suppressing a wounded spirit is akin to concealing an illness and neglecting to seek medical attention. It is beneficial to confide in someone about your troubles. Approach someone who can help, potentially a professional specializing in your specific concern. As Psalm 55:22 advises, "Cast your cares upon the Lord," emphasizing the value of sharing and seeking support for emotional burdens.

Replace it. Find something of better value or meaning in life to replace the past. This is where forgiveness comes in. It may mean you are confronting the source of the problem, perhaps through mediation. Sometimes, this may require you to make things right with God because of what you did wrong. It means taking responsibility for your part. When you do that, you are building a bridge into the future.

Embrace it. Hold on to your newly found value. Some people make resolutions but fail to follow through.

Reframe it. In the context of problem-solving, reframing involves adopting a new perspective and using it as the lens through which you approach similar challenges in the future. Essentially, when you've successfully navigated a situation in the past, framing allows you to use that experience as a guide for resolving similar issues that may arise. It signifies the application of newfound wisdom, recognizing that your ability to handle challenges has evolved, providing a valuable resource for future problem-solving endeavors.

Bring about a broader and more accurate picture of your past by seeing it in its wider context. As Rick Tibbits says, "The larger the context, the more accurate the perspective you will have to help you forgive and heal."[141] Contextualize the words someone currently utters by considering a broader perspective. Assess whether their current statement aligns with their past expressions. What may seem negative or wrong at the moment might be less severe when viewed considering their previous positive remarks. Evaluating their present words in the context of their past affirmations can provide a more nuanced understanding of the situation. Negative things that happen to us should be seen as part of a positive big picture. You look at the forest, not at the trees.

Attitudes of Forgiving Families

In Colossians 3:12-13 we read: *"Therefore, as the elect of God, holy and beloved, put on tender mercies, kindness, humility, meekness, longsuffering; bearing with one another, and forgiving one another, if anyone has a complaint against another; even as Christ forgave you, so you also must do."*

If we are going to forgive, the text above says we must have the following attitudes and attributes:

➤ *Tender mercy*—being gentle toward one another.

➤ *Kindness*—having a soft spot for other people.

➤ *Humility*—having the spirit of compromise, not having to stand your ground all the time.

➤ *Meekness*—not being defensive or feeling hurt when corrected.

➤ *Longsuffering*—giving people time to work things out and to grow.

---

[141] Rick Tibbits with Steve Halliday, *Forgive to Live* (Nashville, TN: Integrity Publishers, 2006), p. 116.

➤ *Bearing with one another*—enduring and putting up with one another.

➤ *Forgiving one another*—willingness to let go and clearing a way forward in the relationship.

Another Scripture that speaks about the importance of forgiveness is Proverbs 25:21-22: *"If your enemy is hungry, give him bread to eat; And if he is thirsty, give him water to drink; For so you will heap coals of fire on his head, And the Lord will reward you"* (NKJV). This scripture encourages us to focus on the other person's needs rather than on his/her faults. In this case the victim, instead of reacting to the negative behavior, responds to the need, with the intent to help the wrongdoer to become a better person. In other words, we should reflect God's attitude toward sinners. He responds with the intent to help sinners experience the future. In God's view, what we can become is more important than what we are. God invests in our future. This is why He forgives and why we, too, should forgive.

APPLICATION: Why is forgiveness essential for the survival of human, marriage, and family relationships? How is unforgiveness detrimental to one's health?

Chapter 9

DELICATE ISSUES IN RELATIONSHIPS

"Men save their best for the workplace and reserve leftovers for the home." Chuck Swindoll

In this concluding chapter, we delve into a range of sensitive issues within relationships, encompassing aspects such as marriage in middle years, parenting and step-parenting, blended families, the impact of divorce on children, dating, and navigating the complexities of singleness. Termed "delicate" due to their intricate and sensitive nature, these issues may not be as openly discussed as others, yet they significantly influence the quality of life and relationships. African families in the diaspora, in particular, frequently grapple with these challenges, highlighting their pervasive and impactful nature.

Marriages in Middle Years

Middle years (35-65 years) can be a time of mixed feelings and competing experiences:

➤ Time to relax when one's goals are achieved.

➤ Time of thanksgiving since the journey has been endured.

➤ Time of looking back at overcoming fearful youthfulness.

➤ Time to bring new pressures and new challenges.

➤ Time when income reaches a peak.

➤ Time to mourn lost opportunities— "I wish I had . . ."

➤ Time to yearn for a young body and freedom from the grind.

➤ Time of generativity or stagnation.

➤ Time to start new careers—flexible ones.

How one approaches the emotions and encounters during the middle years can be the determining factor between success and defeat. The conflict between the past and the current reality often leads to feelings of discouragement. Additionally, there is a common inclination during middle years to relax one's guard in marital relationships, potentially taking them for granted. It's important to recognize that past achievements don't always ensure ongoing success, as love may wane over time. The biblical example of the church at Ephesus serves as a poignant lesson in this context.

God's message to the church at Ephesus was: "*Nevertheless I have this against you, that you have left your first love*" (Rev. 2:4, NKJV). At the time of Paul, the Ephesian church's relationship with Jesus was very remarkable and commendable. Even Paul wrote a report saying: "*Ever since I first heard of your strong <u>faith</u> in the Lord Jesus and your <u>love</u> for God's people everywhere*" (Eph. 1:15 NLT). Thirty years later, as documented in the book of Revelation by John, the state of the church at Ephesus had undergone a transformation. The graph of love had significantly declined. It took three decades for the church to lose its fervor and affection for Jesus, marking a metaphorical middle point in its enduring relationship with Christ.

Ephesus' relationship with Jesus in Revelation is a good example of what happens in African marriages in the diaspora. Typically, marriages that commence on a positive note back home in Africa may undergo transformations once families relocate to the diaspora. Over time, the demands of hectic schedules and various pressures often lead to a gradual erosion of the guardrails. This shift is often propelled by a sense of self-confidence and complacency. The pursuit of economic stability and the constant burden of managing numerous bills tend to overshadow the importance of nurturing family relationships. After the initial excitement of the honeymoon years settles, couples commonly shift their focus towards career commitments, parenting responsibilities, and societal concerns, often neglecting the crucial aspect of intimacy. Much like the church at Ephesus, they become engrossed in the good aspects of life, inadvertently losing sight of what is truly the best in the process.

Another caveat to this is that many couples enjoy marital satisfaction before the children arrive and after they have left home. In other words, intimacy may reach a low point during parenting years and then increase as the adolescents leave home. Children are wonderful human beings, but raising them saps all the energy and resources that parents have. The arrival of a baby changes everything, including schedules, the size of the apartment or house, the size of the car, the distance from the right school, the furniture inside the house, and a lot of other things.

This dynamic suggests the potential for financial strain as couples may find themselves investing in activities they may not afford. Nevertheless, the middle years can offer a valuable period of gratitude, marking a stage where youth is behind, and the potential for productivity or stagnation lies ahead. It is a juncture where the body undergoes changes, acting differently than it did before. These years might be tinged with regret if certain goals remain unfulfilled, yet they also harbor the prospect of transformation, presenting an opportunity for a fresh career path and a rekindling of love with one's spouse.

How should couples strengthen their marriage in the middle years? Here are some suggestions:

> Establishing early priorities in marriage is essential, following this order: God, spouse, children, parents, siblings, extended

family, and friends. While this cultural shift might pose challenges for Africans, it can be argued that a healthy marriage ensures the well-being and happiness of everyone involved. Putting God first includes activities such as the family worshipping together, praying, studying the Bible, returning tithes, giving offerings, having regular church attendance, and involvement in the mission and ministries of the church. This may sound preachy, but it is our experience that putting God first clears the mind of stress and improves one's temperament.

➤ Pay close attention to early warning signs of marital issues, including nagging, insecurity, disrespect, tight-fistedness, criticism, and personal discontent. Avoid keeping issues bottled up; instead, prioritize open communication. Sweeping problems under the rug can have long-term and costly consequences.

➤ Never allow personal goals to compete. Go for what is feasible and sustainable, and be flexible.

➤ Maintain a positive daily life together. Sexual activity does not come naturally in the middle years. This is often the Achilles' Hill for many middle-aged couples. Keeping your marriage happy prevents infidelity. Get professional help.

➤ Instead of contemplating a change in partners, consider a lifestyle change. Exiting a marriage in search of a spark and energy from another source may not be the solution, as challenges exist in various relationships.

New Mother and Baby Blues

Becoming new parents poses distinct challenges for immigrant couples, particularly when comparing the support systems available in Africa to those in the diaspora. In Africa, hiring help for household tasks is more accessible, while in the diaspora, reliance on daycare becomes necessary, often proving to be financially burdensome. This situation often leads to new mothers having to stay at home to care for their children. A personal example is when our grandchildren, Lauren and Michael, were born in Detroit, Michigan. We traveled two hundred miles to offer support through babysitting, given the parents' other commitments. Similarly, when another grandchild, Nathan, was born in Atlanta, Georgia, we had to make occasional trips from Michigan to assist with the demands of childcare.

The support of family members is always a blessing, especially during demanding schedules. Consider the challenges faced by thousands of young parents in the diaspora who do not have the privilege of having parents nearby to help. According to Eisenberg, Murkoff, and Hathway, "There's no other job as emotionally and physically taxing as mothering in the first year. The strain and pressure are not limited to eight hours a day or five days a week, and there are no lunch hours or coffee breaks to spell relief."[142] Another author states that "at the same time, children do not arrive with an owner's manual that tells their parents all they need to do to care for them and how to troubleshoot any problems that may arise. Even experienced parents are sometimes stumped by the actions, words, or attitudes of their children."[143]

The complexity of the situation extends beyond the time demands of caring for a child; it also involves navigating the challenges of parenting skills. Even if parents strive to follow guidelines, there is uncertainty about whether their actions will yield the desired outcomes. The new and young mother often grapples with mild depression stemming from the difficulties of caring for the child, the post-birth healing process, and hormonal changes. This period can strain the marital relationship as the husband may feel sidelined, given the constant attention required by the baby. Adjusting to culturally different roles, such as diaper-changing, cooking, laundry, and other tasks, may be uncomfortable for the husband,

[142] Arlene Eisenberg, Heidi Murkoff and Sandee Hathway, *What to expect When You are Expecting* (New York: Workman Publishing, 1996), p. 575.
[143] Clifford R. Goldstein, ed., Family Seasons, Adult Sabbath School Bible Study Guide, April-June (Nampa, Idaho: Pacific Press Publishing Association, 2019), p. 25.

especially when performed in the presence of friends. This necessitates a rewiring of perspectives to embrace these challenges comfortably.

Situations like these can lead to a decline in the quality of marital relations. It becomes crucial for the couple to have a support network of friends and family to alleviate the pressure, stress, exhaustion, and fatigue. These challenging feelings are not exclusive to new mothers; experienced mothers also undergo similar struggles. The personal experience of Peggie, facing postpartum depression and panic disorder while her premature baby was in an incubator, highlights the importance of seeking medical treatment and the extended healing process involved.

Parenting Crisis

The challenges associated with parenting commence even before children are born and persist throughout their upbringing until they eventually leave home. Ron and Nancy Rockey identified conditions that give rise to feelings of rejection in children:[144]

> ➢ *Forceps delivery.* When the baby is born, pulling the head may produce anger issues.

> ➢ *Cesarean delivery.* When the baby is born through c-section, such babies love being touched.

> ➢ *Late in life baby.* When parents have a baby late in life, it causes relational distance between parent and child.

> ➢ *Less bonding at birth.* When a baby was not expected and came in as an intruder.

> ➢ *Wrong sex.* Children born out of wedlock don't receive the benefit of both parents.

---

[144] Ron and Nancy Rockey, "Binding the Wounds" in Lifestyle Renewal institute, (2000), p. 7.

➤ *Fighting between parents.* This traumatizes children and makes them feel insecure. Sometimes, they feel they are the cause.

➤ *Childhood abuse.* This damages the child psychologically, emotionally, socially, and physically.

➤ *Children left alone too often.* The child grows up feeling unwanted and uncared for.

➤ *Affection or praise based on performance.* This is love based on works. The child feels if he/she doesn't perform, there will be no praise.

For many parents, these things send chills down the spine and make you wish to start over again.

Years ago, we attended George Barna's presentation at Andrews University, Berrien Springs, Michigan. As a guru in family-related research, George Barna described the parenting crises of the times to be:

➤ Morality with no absolutes

➤ Education with no values

➤ Relationships that are short-lived due to divorce

➤ Heroes replaced by celebrities

➤ Physical and emotional challenges due to lack of exercise and proper diet

➤ Spiritual challenges where children are allowed to choose the deity they want because all faiths are equal.

➤ Being spiritual but not religious

On the question of who is responsible for raising children, Barna stated: "Not government, not schools, not churches, but parents." He characterized parenting strategies as default options involving tactics like avoidance, evasion, trial and error, and the absence of a manual, where success is essentially defined as survival. According to his perspective, incorporating Biblical principles into parenting becomes an essential and revolutionary guideline for effective parenting.

In a similar vein, G. Curtis Jones relates a situation where, after a lecture by the late Chicago educator Francis Wayland Parker, a woman asked: "How early can I begin the education of my child?" To this, Parker asked: "When will your child be born?" The woman replied: "Why, he is already five years old." Parker then retorted: "My goodness, woman, don't stand here talking to me – hurry home; already you have lost the first five years."[145]

In Barna's perspective, parenting priorities should revolve around placing God at the center of life. He sees parenting as an act of God, a service to God, and a gift to the child. According to him, the parenting journey should commence from the moment children are born, and some even argue before their birth. Barna highlights that values start developing at the age of nine, and relationships begin shaping at the age of thirteen. It is crucial for parents to be intentional in tailoring the parenting process to each child, identifying teachable moments, and establishing non-negotiable boundaries. These boundaries may include emphasizing the importance of telling the truth, respecting others, controlling speech, accepting punishment, excelling in school, actively pursuing faith, enforcing curfew, and setting clear limits.

Barna challenged parents to behave like parents, remembering that parenting is not a democracy but a benign dictatorship. Parents should own the role, control their temper, be patient, learn to let off steam after children get under their skin, explain their reasons, and listen again and again. It is crucial for parents to comprehend the context of their children's thoughts, recognizing that children may not always express themselves articulately, and sometimes, the unspoken

---

[145] G. Curtis Jones, p. 113.

messages carry significant importance. Parents should exemplify the behaviors they wish to see in their children. Ultimately, parenting is identified as the primary and dominant role in life, with parents serving as the principal life coaches for their children.

When tailoring the parenting process for each child, it's beneficial for parents to pay attention to the child's stages of development. Each developmental stage necessitates a distinct type of relationship with the parents. Seeking wisdom from God becomes crucial for parents to make the necessary adjustments as life coaches in guiding their children through these stages. As the book of Proverbs states: *"Train up a child in the way he should go: and when he is old, he will not depart from it."* Prov. 22:6, KJV. In a nutshell, these are stages of development that show the child's needs and can also help a parent guide a child in the direction they should go.

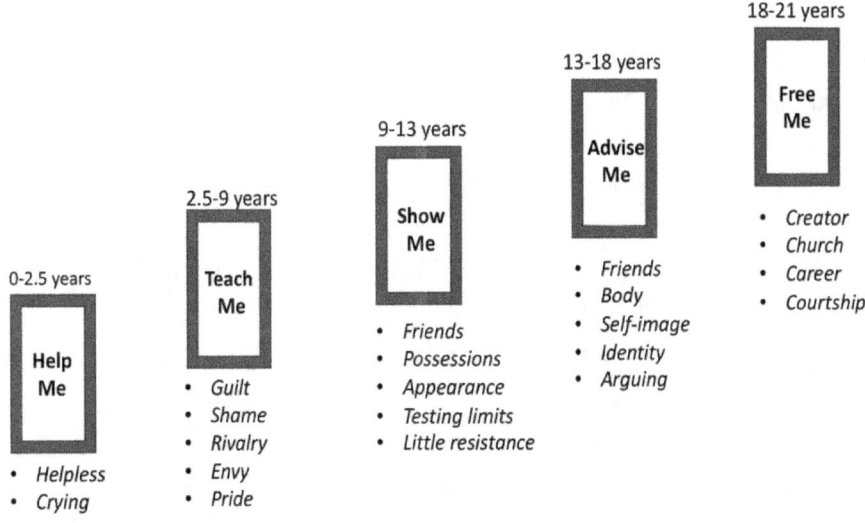

Diagram 9. Stages of Development

One critical yet often overlooked stage in a child's development is the first three years, a period where attention is sometimes diverted toward later years concerning children's behaviors and decisions. The premise is that behaviors and decisions exhibited later in life may have roots in the formative experiences of the first three years.

Recent insights from Suzanne Venker, who actively addresses parents on the potential harm of sending babies and toddlers to daycare, shed light on the historical context. She noted that during the 1970s, the feminist movement significantly influenced women to engage in work outside the home, like men. Venker pointed out that daycare was portrayed as harmless by the feminist movement to encourage women's workforce participation. This observation prompts a reconsideration of the impact of early childhood experiences and the choices made during that crucial developmental period.

In her online article "Will America Ever Be Ready for the Truth about Daycare?" posted February 1, 2012, Suzanne Venker wrote: "Even one of America's premier child psychologists, Dr. Stanley Greenspan, says America has struggled to improve daycare for 20 years – to no avail. The only way it can be improved . . . is for parents to provide most of the care for their children. That way, there would be fewer people using daycare, and perhaps then the system could have a fighting chance. The smaller a business is, the more effective it will be. And make no mistake: Daycare is a business."[146]

The underlying concept is that smaller numbers of children in daycare would allow for more individual attention to each child. Conversely, larger numbers of children in daycare create challenges for caregivers to provide personalized attention to each child due to the increased workload.

In the second video (*The ridiculous idea that daycare is perfectly harmless*), Venker cited five myths about daycare: (1) That there is no right or wrong. This makes daycare appear like a benign choice, something normal. It's all about choice. However, Venker observes that babies need their parents. Even mothers' bodies tell them that they need their babies, (2) That if you meet the physical needs of the child, it is enough. However, the truth is that children need attachment, not just changing their diapers. Children need one primary attachment figure to bond. When children cry, they need immediate attention, which they cannot

---

[146] Suzanne Venker, Will America Ever Be Ready for the Truth about Daycare? Posted online February 1, 2012. Accessed September 15, 2023.

get in a large group of children where there is too much noise. When there is no person specially assigned to them (mother, father, grandma, or nanny), children get stressed (3) That when mom is happy, the child is happy too. The truth, says Venker, is that children don't care about their moms being happy. All they care about is their own happiness. When they are not happy, they get into all kinds of behaviors. (4) That daycare gives children an educational advantage. Contrary to conventional beliefs, Venker highlights that the paramount foundation for a child during the early years is emotional development, with education being their least essential requirement. Additionally, she challenges the notion that daycare is highly beneficial for socialization. Venker argues that socialization plays a negligible role in the first four years of a child's life, as babies typically engage in parallel play, merely playing alongside others without substantial emotional interaction.

The concerns raised by Suzanne Venker merit careful consideration from every family, especially those with babies and toddlers. While individual family circumstances may vary, the fundamental assertion remains significant – the home is deemed as the optimal environment for early childhood development. Ellen G. While concurs: "Parents should not permit business cares, worldly customs and maxims, and fashion to have a controlling power over them so that they neglect their children in babyhood and fail to give their children proper instruction as they increase in years."[147]

Teaching Values to the Young

One of the great challenges in our world today is the disappearance of values as we know them among our children and young people. The phrase "Kids these days" frequently emerges from the mouths of frustrated and disappointed adults, signaling a perceived erosion of traditional values that once bound communities and societies together. There appears to be a collective struggle to find effective strategies to

---

[147] Ellen G. White, *The Adventist Home*, online version, page 183. Accessed September 15, 2023.

reinstate these old values. Furthermore, contemporary public discourse questions the necessity of values in an era marked by free speech and expression. This debate has created divisions among adults, with some advocating for values neutrality, asserting that values are relative and should be individually determined. Unfortunately, this stance has left children and young people in a state of confusion, lacking a clear sense of identity. Then there are those who believe that only consensus values (those widely embraced) need to be communicated, especially in public schools. Acknowledging the division within communities regarding a range of values, some individuals propose teaching only those values that enjoy consensus. These commonly accepted values include truthfulness, respect, kindness, responsibility, liberty, equality, and justice.

In a previous discussion, we explored three interdependent institutions—the home, the church, and the school (specifically, a Christian school). Among these, the home assumes the most central role as it establishes the foundation for moral development, with truth serving as a fundamental basis. The church and school then function as crucial support systems. The family acts as a bridge, connecting the church and the school in the collective effort to foster moral and ethical values in individuals.

This being the case, the range of values is broader than the consensus values just mentioned above. Therefore, values should consider the family's, the church's, and the school's belief systems and include the moral, spiritual, physical, emotional, and intellectual dimensions of life.[148] It's crucial to highlight that the teaching of values should not only be conveyed through instruction but also demonstrated through the actions of those in authoritative roles. The adage, "values are caught and not taught," emphasizes the importance of modeling values in addition to verbal instruction. Effective moral education involves a harmonious combination of explicit teaching and consistent, exemplary behavior from authority figures.

---

[148] George Barna, *Transforming children into Spiritual Champions* (Ventura, CA: Regal Books, 2003), p. 53.

Step-Parenting and Blended Families

Due to the complexities of human relationships and our inherent brokenness, blended families and step-parenting have become increasingly prevalent. A blended family, also known as a stepfamily, reconstituted family, or complex family, is formed when one or both parents have children from a previous relationship. The circumstances leading to a blended family can vary, including experiences such as an extramarital affair, the death of a spouse, divorce, remarriage, out-of-wedlock relationships, or guardianship of children from an extended family due to the death of parents. In each case, a child is raised by someone who is not their biological father or mother. Step-parenting can pose significant challenges if not approached thoughtfully.

From an African cultural perspective, the term "stepparent" is not commonly used. In African cultures, children are typically expected to refer to a stepparent as "father" or "mother" as appropriate. This intentional choice aims to assimilate the children into the new family relationship and aligns with the broader African cultural norm where children are expected to address any adult of their parent's age as "father" or "mother." Even the siblings of one's parent are addressed using these titles. While these cultural norms may influence relationship dynamics, it's important to note that relying solely on such titles does not always serve as a solution to the challenges that can arise in marital relationships.

Alfred R. Jones observes that even in the West, the word "stepfamily" has a negative connotation that suggests shame, broken homes, and deprivation.[149] The merging of two families can give rise to conflicting emotions among ex-spouses. As someone caught in the crossfire between the new spouse and children and the persistent involvement of the ex-spouse, navigating these dynamics can be challenging. Contrary to the assumption that being married to their mother or father automatically

---

[149] Alfred Jones, pp. 85-94. Jones presents this in the context of the stepfather. However, it applies to both.

confers parental status, stepparents may encounter resistance from children who instinctively reject the newcomer.

There may be a temptation to apply the same standards used in raising biological children to stepchildren, potentially leading to judgment. It's crucial to remember that any criticism of stepchildren is, in essence, a criticism of the new spouse. Given the sensitivity of this matter, Jones proposes considerations for parents in handling such situations.

➢ Recognize the differences between a first family and a stepfamily.

➢ Embrace your new role as a stepparent. Help and allow children time to adjust.

➢ Keep lines of communication open among all family members, remembering that conflicts are an opportunity for growth.

➢ Recognize and mourn the losses that trouble each member.

➢ Resolve conflicts with your spouse and ex-spouse about money, discipline, and visitation.

➢ Encourage and show love to reduce feelings of jealousy and competition.

➢ Enforce discipline without creating more animosity.

➢ Lessen feelings of rejection, insecurity, and guilt among all members.

➢ Bond together to experience the joys of being family.

Divorce and its Effects

The perspective mentioned here draws on a scientific understanding that humans, due to their innate drive for procreation, may be born with certain predispositions, often referred to as "selfish genes." This idea suggests that our evolutionary history has shaped us in ways that prioritize survival and reproduction, potentially leading to self-centered tendencies. The implication is that these inherent qualities can make it challenging for individuals to think unemotionally and make consistently good choices. This perspective aligns with certain evolutionary theories that examine the impact of genetics on human behavior. It's important to note that this is one perspective within the broader landscape of scientific and philosophical discussions on human nature and decision-making. In the Bible, David says, "Behold, I was shapen in iniquity; and in sin did my mother conceive me" (Ps. 51:5, KJV). It can truly be said that when each spouse falls apart, the marriage falls apart. In other words, a marriage breaks down because of spouses who individually had fallen apart prior to their getting into marriage.

This viewpoint underscores the recognition that individuals entering marriage are not perfect; they bring with them various challenges and imperfections. Before marriage, people may have already experienced physical, spiritual, emotional, and social struggles. This perspective acknowledges that individuals seek medical attention, grapple with their spiritual connection, and deal with emotional issues such as anger, anxiety, fears, and doubts before entering marriage. Additionally, tensions with parents and siblings may also be part of the pre-marital experience. The overall notion is that individuals come into marriage with a certain degree of brokenness and imperfection.

Marriage is not an institution in which strong, perfect, and healthy people come together. It is an institution where couples recognize their weaknesses and imperfections. We bring our historical, cultural, societal, and temperamental baggage. For this reason, Paul described human struggle: *"For I know that in me (that is in my flesh) nothing good dwells; for to will is present with me, but how to perform what is good I do not find. For the good that I will to do, I do not do; but the evil I will not to do, that I practice"* (Rom 7:18-19, NKJV). Because of this, we learn to depend on God's grace as we walk the journey together in marriage. When we are aware of our premarital brokenness, we are more likely to become patient, tolerant, humble, and confessional in the marriage relationship.

Indeed, it's important to acknowledge the existence of wrong marriages. These are unions where two individuals who are already grappling with their own brokenness enter matrimony for misguided reasons. Such reasons may include seeking material or financial support, responding to an out-of-wedlock pregnancy, pursuing prestige associated with being married to a celebrity or aligning with values that are fundamentally in conflict. Another aspect is marrying someone with known deep-seated character issues or engaging with a partner who exhibits traits like unfaithfulness, lack of love, uncooperativeness, lack of sympathy, or untrustworthiness. Without the intervention of divine grace, these attitudes can serve as fertile ground for marital challenges and, in some cases, lead to emotional divorce.

Factors involving divorce among Africans are quite often complicated by cultural paraphernalia. George Phiri observes:

> In Africa, when divorce occurs, it is usually a husband who divorces a wife. The one who marries another is responsible for divorce. Wives also propose divorce where the husband fails to fulfill his marital duties, such as having sex with his wife for a prolonged period without genuine reasons, such as sickness. Irresponsibility of the husband to fend for the household is another reason for an African woman to seek divorce from her husband, though this is difficult in Africa because most women are not yet breadwinners. Further, battering is another reason for women to seek divorce from their husbands . . . In addition, in the African context, a man is expected to fend for his wife and

the entire household. He shoulders the responsibility of fathering an extended family community. In other words, the African traditions give a husband more powers and responsibilities over a wife, though this trend is diminishing in modern African societies due to gender rights, influences of the contemporary social, economic, and political world, and so forth . . ."[150]

In Western society, divorce has its own cultural trappings. Even though divorce is the most devastating experience that can ever happen to any family, it has become an easily acceptable option when solving marital problems. Even though the costs are high, couples opt out of wedlock, like exchanging cars. Along this line, Theodora Ooms said we should "make marriage better to be in rather than more difficult to get out of."[151] Perhaps we can reword it differently: We should make marriage better to get in, better to remain in, and reasonable to not get out of.

When couples assess their relationship, they often employ the principles of cost-benefit analysis or draw upon the social exchange theory from social psychology. The social exchange theory posits that self-interest is a fundamental driver in human interactions, suggesting that individuals aim to maximize benefits while minimizing costs in their decision-making processes. Applied to the context of divorce, this theory implies that individuals contemplating divorce will evaluate the potential benefits against the associated risks. If the perceived risks outweigh the benefits, the couple may choose to pursue divorce.

Weigh the costs of investing money, time, and effort into the relationship against the benefits derived from aspects such as friendship, companionship, and social support. If the rewards of staying in the marriage surpass the costs of potential divorce, the preference may be to remain in the relationship. However, if the costs significantly outweigh the benefits, an individual may initiate divorce proceedings.

---

[150] George Allan Phiri, pp. 126-127.
[151] Quoted in Paul Peachey, Leaving and Cleaving, p. 171.

Unfortunately, when couples decide on costs over benefits, they always overlook the fact that the effects of divorce cannot be measured mathematically; they are devastating and should not be underestimated. The spouses themselves suffer, having to deal with the following issues:

➢ Dealing with the feelings of frustration, despair, disappointment, rejection, and estrangement.

➢ Dealing with the loss of the relatives of your spouse and having to change social networks.

➢ Dealing with the legal, economic, parental, and psychological issues because of divorce.

➢ Dealing with the stigma of being seen as socially, morally, and psychologically deviant.

➢ Dealing with the blame game like ping pong to influence relatives and friends to take sides.

➢ Dealing with the haunting attitudes of selfishness, hostility, and vindictiveness.

The effects of divorce have a devastating impact on children as well. Kern P. Tobias says the couple will often choose to stay married, telling themselves that "a lousy marriage is better than a good divorce.[152] According to Tobias,[153] children of divorced parents experience challenges in several following ways:

➢ Dealing with a personal sense of insecurity that stands in the way of sustaining good relationships.

---

[152] Kern P. Tobias, "Exploring the impact of a marriage seminar on marital relationships in the Seventh-day Adventist Church in Trinidad," D. Min. diss. Andrews University, Berrien Springs, Michigan, 2010, p. 31.
[153] See Tobias, pp. 31-40.

➢ Dealing with the way they raise their own children, especially when divorce is pursued in anger.

➢ Dealing with the sense of guilt of having caused the divorce.

➢ Dealing with the feeling that the remaining parent will leave also.

➢ Dealing with the anger caused by the way their parents have acted.

➢ Dealing with the issues of failing to cope with their classes at school.

➢ Dealing with the experience of poverty and marginalization that human society often creates.

Children of divorced parents often grapple with the traumatic experience of moving back and forth between their parent's homes. It's important to recognize that these children may struggle to articulate their emotions due to unresolved grief, and their feelings may manifest through expressions of denial, anger, sadness, fantasy, withdrawal, rebellion, or other behaviors.

In African cultural settings, extended family support traditionally plays a significant role in providing broader assistance to children of divorced parents. However, families in the diaspora may not always have access to such extended support systems. Consequently, they must navigate the challenge of raising children under the custody of one parent while the other parent has visitation rights according to legal arrangements. This constant transition can place children in a state of psychological dilemma. Moreover, the ability to instill values of love and forgiveness may be compromised, as parents are perceived to have failed to demonstrate these values through the divorce process.

According to Paul Peachey, children are apprentices under two former biologically unrelated strangers, now parents. When the parents separate, the apprenticeship aborts.[154] This underscores the idea that marriage entails a stewardship responsibility, where parents are accountable not only to each other but, more significantly, to their children. When a couple says, "I do," they are not just committing to each other but are also entering into a covenant to bear the responsibility of raising their children.

Permanent Cohabitation

Types of marriage practices in Africa include (1) *monogamy*—being married to one person at a time, (2) *polygamy*—being married to more than one person at the same time, (3) *endogamy*—marriage within one's community, clan, or tribe, (4) *homogamy*—from same gender, sociological, or educational background), and (5) *cohabitation*—living together as a couple without being married. While monogamy is generally the dominant view of marriage, certain cultures and even governments expand marriage to include polygamy. Even though polygamy is not relationally and economically sustainable today, it is still allowed in many parts of Africa, for example, Eswatini (Swaziland).

While homogamy (same-gender marriage) may not be widely accepted in many African cultures, it is openly practiced and legally recognized in countries like South Africa. In the West, there is increasing acceptance of this practice, with more people being open to it and governments acknowledging it as a human rights issue. The cultural and legal landscape regarding same-gender marriage varies across different regions and societies.

Culturally, in Africa, permanent cohabitation has sometimes been granted marriage status even though it is not officially legalized. The government's general guideline has been that if stability in long-term cohabitation is evident, individuals in such a relationship may be considered married. This policy has occasionally led to tension between families, particularly when the woman's family insists on the payment of lobola (bride price), which the man's family might find challenging to afford. The church, too, has found itself in a dilemma in

---

[154] Paul Peachey, *Living and Clinging*, p. 94.

such situations, often having to recognize such practices as constituting a form of marriage. The dynamics of recognizing relationships as marriages can vary and may present challenges, particularly when cultural and religious traditions intersect with legal definitions.

In Western cultures, permanent cohabitation has become acceptable because of the benefits it offers, such as:

➢ Freedom to walk in and out of the relationship without any legal commitments, except where children and property are involved.

➢ Economic benefits as it relates to payment of bills such as rent, etc.

➢ Social advantages like warding off loneliness from being single and living alone.

➢ Psychological purposes of dealing with peer pressure and stereotypes surrounding singleness.

Apart from the above seeming benefits, cohabitation has shocking revelations. In his report on the Study on Faith & Relationships (cited in the introduction), J. P. De Gance outlines a number of issues faced by cohabitors, such as the following:[155]

➢ A church going cohabiting man is 53 percent more likely to report struggling in his relationship than a married man. A cohabiting woman is 73 percent more likely than a married woman.

➢ A cohabiting man in his 30s is 77 percent more likely to report struggling in his relationship than a married man in the same age group.

---

[155] J. P. De Gance, p. 12.

➢ Cohabitors have much higher levels of sexual infidelity than married partners. Besides, they are more likely to break up than marrieds.

➢ A cohabiting woman is more likely to experience intimate partner violence and domestic violence than a married woman.

➢ Cohabiting is also more dangerous and unsafe for children.

Unfortunately, the absence of government laws preventing cohabitation has led many individuals to engage in this practice, as it lacks defined rituals or specific requirements, allowing couples to establish their own terms. The church faces a significant challenge in addressing cohabitation, as while the Bible and church standards condemn the practice, enforcing these standards proves difficult. Publicly discussing someone's name for disciplinary purposes can lead to potential lawsuits, creating a reluctance to intervene directly.

Despite these challenges, the church should not be discouraged from actively engaging with the issue. According to Phiri, suggested approaches include collaborating with interest groups advocating for government intervention, discouraging cohabitation among church members, offering direct counseling to those involved, allowing the gospel to inspire change and formalizing relationships through marriage, and providing premarital counseling to young people before they engage in the practice. Instead of making pronouncements from the pulpit, addressing the issue through interactive settings such as seminars or small group discussions may be more effective, particularly with resistant young adults.

"Evangelistic" Dating

You may be wondering what is meant by evangelistic dating. "Evangelistic" dating does not mean dating a person to make him/her a Christian so you can marry them. What we mean is that God will not give you a perfect date. God may guide you to someone who complements your personality. However, when dating, it's crucial to ensure that the person you choose will be a positive influence on the next person who might date them if your relationship doesn't work out. Initial impressions might reveal certain aspects of their personality that seem unpleasant, but with time, both individuals may adjust to the Christian way the dating is conducted. Responsible dating involves maintaining honesty, cleanliness, and a Christ-like approach. It recognizes that everyone has imperfections, and dating is meant for individuals with the goal of committing to a lifelong relationship.

One young man dated a lady from another faith. He did not know what to do about the potential conflict that might result from a marital relationship where two people practiced different faiths. Instead of him trying to directly convert her to his faith, he decided to have her enroll in long distance of Voice of Prophecy Bible studies. She chose to enroll in faith-based studies, and after completing them, she made a personal decision to be baptized and join his faith. Subsequently, they entered marriage, had children, and enjoyed a happy married life during their retirement years. This approach requires patience to allow the process to unfold naturally, avoiding the perception of being rushed or making a convenient change solely for the purpose of marrying someone.

Another good example of evangelistic dating is the story of Miguel Manuel Mafugula of Mozambique. He was in tenth grade at the age of 21. Adelina, a 16-year-old grade seven girl, asked for his help with her homework. In the process, she shared with him a Bible text in Exodus 20 about keeping the Sabbath. Consequently, he eventually chose to undergo baptism. He pursued a career as a chemistry teacher and later entered marriage with Adelina. The motivations behind Adelina seeking Miguel's help with homework and sharing that Bible text remain unknown, but the outcomes exceeded her initial expectations.

The point we are making here is that dating involves courage, faith, and risk. Courage means avoiding distancing yourself at first sight and getting acquainted with the other person until you see clearly what makes that person tick. Faith means trusting the Holy Spirit to guide you so that you can lend a positive influence on the other person to help him/her make genuine changes in their life. Risk means that you can never know the outcome of your courage and faith. At some point, you should be prepared to walk away when you see red lights flushing. But even at that point, parting ways can be celebrated because the dating was clean.

Dating is the phase during which individuals get to know each other before marriage. The underlying idea is that young people need the chance to assess their compatibility with various individuals to determine who can best fulfill their needs and bring them happiness. However, dating has evolved to the point where the original purpose of finding a potential marriage partner is often overlooked. It has transitioned into a recreational activity rather than a pursuit of a long-term goal. Consequently, it often initiates in secondary or high school and extends into the college years. This is a trial and error that can cause many problems, such as:[156]

➤ Leading to intimacy but not necessarily to commitment. For example, when you allow someone to kiss you, it means that that person will possibly kiss another person.

➤ Tending to skip the "friendship" stage and rush into a serious relationship.

➤ Mistaking a physical relationship for love.

➤ Isolating a couple from other vital relationships, especially if the friendship stages are skipped.

➤ Distracting the mind from the primary duty of preparing for the future.

➤ Causing discontentment with God's gift of singleness.

➤ Creating an artificial environment for evaluating another person's character.

---

[156] Kamika Guthrie, "Student Movement," Andrews University (March 30, 2005), p. 4.

Numerous issues can be mitigated if individuals prioritize building "friendships" initially rather than fixating on a singular person they consider special and potentially marriage material. Before venturing into a romantic relationship, it's crucial to introspect and ask, "Am I ready for marriage?" Assessing whether you can provide for yourself and your prospective life partner is essential. Additionally, adhering to the Biblical principles discussed in Chapter 4 should serve as a default guide, making religious beliefs a significant factor throughout the friendship and dating process.

Mental Health and the Family

This book is incomplete without addressing the challenge of mental health disorders (psychosis), particularly among children, youth, and young adults, acknowledging that depression transcends age boundaries. The primary objectives are (1) to underscore the significance of mental health concerns, (2) to generate awareness about mental health disorders, and (3) to illustrate the impact of these disorders on African families in the diaspora. It is important to note that these observations are drawn from general perspectives rather than clinical or diagnostic studies.

According to the World Health Organization, mental health is a basic human right that is crucial to personal, community, and socio-economic development. It is a state of mental well-being, allowing one to cope with life's stresses and contribute to the community. It is about how one feels, thinks, and behaves.[157] Mental health disorders impose limitations on one's ability to cope with stressors, making it difficult for one to become productive personally and socially.

Regrettably, numerous young individuals end their lives through suicide, often stemming from undiagnosed and untreated mental health disorders. This profound issue resonates within African families in the diaspora, sparking extensive discussions. These families earnestly

---

[157] World Health Organization, "Mental Health," 17 June 2022. Accessed online August 16, 2023.

strive to comprehend the risk factors, identify symptoms indicative of mental health disorders, and proactively address these challenges to prevent the tragic loss of their children.

Types of mental health disorders vary from one person to another. These include, among others, depression, anxiety disorders, mood disorders, bipolar disorders, Schizophrenia, post-traumatic stress disorders (PTSD), and eating disorders. Tendai Masiriri earned a Ph.D. in interdisciplinary health studies, holds a license in social work, and has worked with governments both in the United States and in Africa on the plight of children. In his presentation at Empowered Men's Ministry (EMM), an African group in North America, Dr. Masiriri identified the following clinical mental health disorders: neurodevelopmental disorders, Schizophrenia spectrum, and other psychotic disorders, mood disorders, anxiety disorders, obsessive-compulsive and related disorders, trauma and stressor-related disorders, dissociative disorders, somatic symptom and related disorders, substance-related and addictive disorders, and personality disorders.[158] While many of these technical scientific terms may go over our heads, it is important to familiarize oneself as well as seek help to understand them.

Dr. Masiriri, in his presentation, clarified that numerous individuals grapple with confusion regarding their emotions and behaviors, often attributing them to external factors or events. He illustrated the intricate interconnection between thoughts, emotions, and behaviors and subsequently delineated unhealthy beliefs and attitudes that manifest as symptoms of mental health disorders:

➢ *Abandonment*: Feeling and thinking that one cannot tolerate being alone and taking extreme measures to keep from being alone.

➢ *Approval seeking*: Feeling of being unlikable or unlovable. Telling oneself that nobody cares about me and failing to keep relationships.

---

[158] Tendai Masiriri, "Rational Self-Counseling for Behavioral Health Disorders," a power point presentation to Empowered Men's Ministry, 2023.

➤ *Emotional deprivation*: Experience of not attempting to meet personal needs and making others' needs more important than one's own.

➤ *Emotional inhibition*: Bottling up thoughts and feelings because they would be unacceptable or harmful.

➤ *Entitlement*: Putting on a façade of being special or better or more deserving than others, yet inwardly insecure.

➤ *Failure*: Telling oneself, "I'm not good enough. Am a loser."

➤ *Helplessness*: Feeling of being powerless, inadequate, and not coping with a situation.

➤ *Insufficient self-control*: Desire to have it now. Instant gratification through substance abuse, promiscuity, and temper.

➤ *Mistrust*: Seeing others as being untrustworthy and being overly suspicious and paranoid.

➤ *Punitive*: Showing sadistic and self-harming behaviors. Directing punishment toward self or others.

➤ *Subjugation*: Controlling others, not self.

➤ *Vulnerability*: Feeling unsafe, overly susceptible to being hurt, and dominated by unrealistic fears.

➤ *Worthlessness/defectiveness*: Feeling unworthy and blaming oneself.

While professional help is necessary to diagnose and treat these disorders, self-help actions can be taken to improve the quality of one's life. Some of these disorders may be a result of childhood experiences, such as being shouted at, having one's achievement ignored, being criticized for not being perfect, and being denied genuine affection.[159]

Nebra Glover Tawwab suggests that "mental health issues can be prompted by our neurological response to stress . . . When we are stressed, our brain has difficulty shutting down. Our sleep is affected. Dread sets in. As a therapist, I observe poor self-care, feelings of being overwhelmed, resentment, avoidance, and other mental health issues as common presentations of boundary issues."[160] Tawwab argues that "the root of self-care is setting boundaries."[161] In other words, when we fail to set boundaries (discussed in chapter 5), we will feel "taken advantage of, frustrated, irritated, annoyed, and bitter."[162] In this regard, boundaries promote mental health in several ways: safeguarding overextending ourselves, practicing self-care, defining roles in our relationships, communicating acceptable and unacceptable behaviors, determining what to expect from others, upholding and communicating our needs, creating healthy relationships, creating clarity, and feeling safe.[163]

Tawwab observes two extreme levels of boundaries that can contribute to mental issues.[164] The first is *porous boundaries* such as oversharing, codependency, too much closeness, pleasing people, fear of rejection, and accepting mistreatment. The second extreme is *rigid boundaries* such as never sharing, building walls, avoiding vulnerability, expecting too much of others, and enforcing strict rules. As said earlier in Chapter 5, *healthy boundaries* must be communicated clearly and followed through with actions.

According to Adam Felman and Rachel Ann Tee-Melegrito, having limited financial means or belonging to a marginalized or persecuted ethnic group can increase the risk of mental and physical health disorders. They cite adverse experiences such as child abuse, parental loss, parental separation, and parental illness as affecting

---

[159]   Casalnnie Henry, *Neutralizing Fear*, p. 51.
[160]   Nebra Glover Tawwab, *Set Boundaries, Find Peace*, p. 5.
[161]   Ibid., p. 6.
[162]   Ibid.
[163]   Ibid., p. 8.
[164]   Ibid., pp. 10-11.

a growing child's mental and physical health.[165] They suggest the following self-care practices to mitigate these disorders and enhance a positive attitude toward self, others, and events:

➢ Doing regular exercise

➢ Eating a balanced diet and staying hydrated

➢ Aiming for good-quality sleep

➢ Performing relaxing activities

➢ Practicing gratefulness

➢ Challenging negative thoughts

➢ Looking for positive social interactions

In Matthew 26:14-16, 20-25, we read about Judas Iscariot and his state of mental health. Jesus had done everything to warn him about his plan to betray Him. But Judas was heedless and unmindful of the consequences of his thoughts and actions. In chapter 27:3-3 (NKJV), we read:

> "Then Judas, His betrayer, seeing that He had been condemned, was remorseful and brought back the thirty pieces of silver to the chief priests and elders, saying, 'I have sinned by betraying innocent blood.' And they said, 'What is that to us? You see to it!' Then he threw down the pieces of silver in temple and departed, and went and hanged himself."

Judas realized that his choices had consequences resulting from anxiety, guilt, and depression. Instead of seeking repentance and

---

[165] Adam Felman and Rachel Ann Tee-Melegrito, "What is Mental Health?" Posted online and updated December 23,2022. Accessed July 20, 2023.

forgiveness, he left the presence of the Forgiver and went on to commit suicide. Unfortunately, this is the recourse that many take to deal with mental health disorders. Our relationship with Jesus promotes a positive self-identity and meaning in life. When we are down to the wire, we know we are not alone. When we are messed up, we know that Jesus will not reject us. He loves us unconditionally. He sees in us what we can become when we surrender our lives to Him.

Bob Phillips addresses the importance of self-care through self-talk. He suggests that one should confront his/her favorite excuses for putting off change. He goes on to outline a list of excuses and asks people to place a check on phrases and excuses they often use to avoid difficult tasks or situations. The following "favorite excuses" are listed by permission from the publisher:[166]

- ○ I'm too busy.

- ○ I'm too old.

- ○ I'm too tired.

- ○ I'm too young.

- ○ I'm doing okay.

- ○ I'm not sure I have the energy.

- ○ I'm really not good at that.

- ○ I'm just not up to it.

- ○ I'm not feeling good.

- ○ I'm not smart enough.

---

[166] Taken from: 42 Days to Feeling Great. Copyright © 2001 by Bob Phillips. Published by Harvest House Publishers, Eugene, Oregon 97408. Used by Permission. See pages 65-68.

○ I'm not comfortable where I'm at.

○ I'm overwhelmed.

○ I'm not that organized.

○ I'm a procrastinator.

○ I'm not cut out for that.

○ I'm quiet by nature.

○ I'm just too lazy.

○ I'm waiting for the right moment.

○ I'm waiting for them to say they are sorry.

○ I don't have the time right now.

○ I don't want to.

○ I can't afford it.

○ I don't have the willpower.

○ I don't have the strength.

○ I don't think I could do it.

○ I don't think it will work.

○ I don't need any more pain.

○ I don't need any more stress.

○ I have better things to do.

○ I don't deserve this.

○ I never have any luck.

○ I don't think I could pull it off.

○ I don't want to work that hard.

○ I don't have any choice.

○ I like it the way it is.

○ I don't want to talk about it.

○ I can't break the habit.

○ I can't help it.

○ I've got too many responsibilities.

○ I've been hurt enough already.

○ I've never been good at anything.

○ I've tried it before, and it doesn't work.

○ I've had it.

○ It won't do any good.

○ It's just my upbringing.

○ It's just my personality.

○ It's not my fault.

○ You just don't understand.

○ You have no idea what I've been going through.

○ Not today.

○ Maybe when I'm feeling better.

○ Leave me alone.

○ Once the kids get out of the home . . .

○ My brain can't handle it now.

○ No one listens to me anyway.

○ Nothing else changes.

○ Why don't you change the subject.

○ Only the rich succeed.

○ No matter what I do. It won't make any difference.

As noted above, confronting one's favorite excuses and fears offers a road map toward self-care.

Single and Happy

Singleness can drive one into a search for identity. A social media story tells about boys who got three goats and marked them number 1, 2, and 4, respectively. At night they let them loose into a school where they messed up the yard. In the morning, school officials found the three goats but goat number 3 was missing. They looked everywhere but could not find goat number 3. The point is that there is temptation to look for what does not exist while ignoring what we already have.

We are familiar with the story of a single man who endured constant teasing from his friends due to his single status. Fortunately, he didn't let the teasing affect him outwardly, though it's possible that it had some impact on his self-esteem in private. Despite the stereotypes and misconceptions that single individuals often face, he has chosen to remain single. According to Alfred Jones, they are perceived as lonely losers looking for companionship.[167] The painful question mostly asked is, "How come a nice man like you isn't married?" In the Ndebele language, they ask, "*Sizakudla nin'inyama?*" This literally means, "When are you going to have a wedding so we can enjoy a feast?" That's how insensitive this can be to a single person.

According to Jones, such treatment causes one to have negative attitudes toward himself.[168] You have a sense of shame. You are bothered by a lot. Society often places various expectations and biases on unmarried individuals, associating them with stereotypes such as irresponsibility, immaturity, unfulfillment, being out of step with God's plan, homosexuality, and abnormality. In certain cultures, like in Africa, the issue of childlessness can also lead to feelings of shame. When we talk about singleness, it's important to note that the category of single people is diverse, encompassing younger singles in their teens, young adult singles, those who have never been married, divorced individuals, separated individuals, widowed individuals, and single parents. They are single for various reasons, such as:

➢ Because they are teens still living at home.

➢ Because they are still looking for the person who fits the values they stand for.

➢ Because they believe God called them to the life of singleness.

➢ Because they have a physical disability that prevents them from getting into a relationship.

---

[167] Alfred Jones, The Black Male's Survival Manual, 1999, p. 97.
[168] Ibid., pp. 98-99.

> ➤ Because a prior relationship didn't work or a vow that didn't hold.

> ➤ Because of the death of a spouse.

African cultures are generally conservative. Conservative individuals often display a tendency toward legalism, which can lack sympathy and foster a blame-oriented mindset. It's crucial to avoid making uninformed judgments about single people and refrain from imposing impractical expectations on them. Instead, there should be an acknowledgment of the challenges that singles face, recognizing them as genuine and complete human beings whose lives deserve celebration, regardless of their past experiences. Understanding the difficulties of managing life as a single person, it is important to extend support and love to one another, trusting that God is in the business of making individuals whole again. Because of the importance and sensitive nature of the issue of singleness, we want to conclude by sharing observations and suggestions that can benefit single people. We are indebted to Alfred Jones for the following observations and suggestions.[169]

Common Mistakes of Singles

The following are mistakes that singles make:

> ➤ Thinking that marriage is the only normal lifestyle and that it will solve all problems

> ➤ Misinterpreting the intentions of the opposite sex

> ➤ Putting too much in a relationship and hanging on too long

> ➤ Failure to read danger signals in a relationship

---

[169] Jones (1999), pp. 102-105 (drawn from Mary Whelchel, 1988.

➢ Getting physically involved and going too far

➢ Thinking that the only necessary requirement for a date or mate is being a Christian.

➢ Judging others too quickly by our list of requirements we carry around

➢ Thinking that anything is better than being alone

➢ Thinking and talking too much about the opposite sex

➢ Fear to share real feelings or express opinions.

➢ Being visually oriented (Revealing excessive openness, vulnerability, and transparency, particularly among women.

➢ Being overly influenced by visual aspects, especially among men, and dismissing potential partners based on appearances.

➢ Fear of lifetimeConcealing emotions to project a stoic, masculine image.

➢ Apprehension about making a lifelong commitment is particularly prevalent among men.

➢ Neglecting the development of genuine friendships with individuals of the opposite gender.

➢ Avoiding associations with people who may not enhance our image.

➢ Marking a distinction from married individuals and avoiding connections with them.

➢ Feeling envy and jealousy towards married individuals.

- ➢ Allowing relationships with married individuals to surpass established boundaries.

- ➢ Permitting negative attitudes from family members to impede relationship-building.

- ➢ Lacking financial planning and budgeting.

- ➢ Excessive spending and succumbing to impulsive desires.

- ➢ Making short-term vision career decisions.

- ➢ Making career decisions is influenced by the desire for an ideal partner, particularly among women.

- ➢ Fearing success in a career, particularly among women.

- ➢ Keeping options open leads to flirtatious behavior.

- ➢ Developing an inflexible, set-in-our-ways mindset.

- ➢ Becoming workaholics to combat loneliness.

- ➢ Living a double life due to a lack of accountability.

- ➢ Not fully utilizing our gifts within the church community.

- ➢ Failing to express hospitality due to fear of being misunderstood.

- ➢ Allowing a relationship to control commitment to Christ.

Maintaining a Good Attitude

Single people need to develop positive attitudes toward themselves, others, and society:[170]

➤ Recognize and appreciate your unique qualities and talents.

➤ Nurture a healthy self-respect and a strong sense of self-worth.

➤ Take accountability for your actions and decisions.

➤ Utilize your talents to diminish any feelings of inferiority.

➤ Set and achieve meaningful goals to experience a sense of accomplishment.

➤ Reinforce your achievements by rewarding yourself.

➤ Redefine loneliness as a state distinct from being alone.

➤ Embrace and appreciate your single status; foster confidence in personal growth.

➤ Refrain from actively seeking the elusive "one and only"; allow relationships to develop naturally.

➤ Cultivate meaningful friendships with individuals of both the same and opposite sex.

➤ Seek connections with supportive and nourishing individuals while avoiding negativity and harm.

➤ View singles as potential friends rather than societal outcasts.

---

[170] Ibid.

- ➢ Accept and embrace all forms of singlehood—divorced, separated, widowed, and never married.

- ➢ Focus on recognizing and celebrating the similarities between men and women.

- ➢ Advocate against any injustices faced by single individuals.

- ➢ Embrace and actively live a fulfilling single life.

- ➢ Promote understanding and goodwill between married and single individuals.

APPLICATION: Identify delicate issues affecting any aspect of your life. What steps are you planning to take to address them? What is the difference between static and dynamic issues?

Conclusion

Paul's letter to the Philippians, written from his prison cell in Rome, reveals his encouragement to people who were free to experience JOY. Despite his confinement, the repeated mention of the words "joy" and "rejoice" underscores the importance of maintaining a positive outlook on life. Paul shares various reasons for this joy, applicable to African families in the diaspora confronting diverse challenges. From a Biblical standpoint, joy is depicted as an internal state of peace and satisfaction that persists despite external adversities. Couples and families can have a positive outlook and create a path forward based on the following reasons from the book of Philippians:

- Those who believe alike as *"partners in the gospel"* (1:5) will stick together. The word "partner" also means "fellowship" or "relationship." The gospel unites families. Those who share the same faith will cling together regardless of what happens around them. When they put God at the top of their priorities, couples can overcome besetting hardships because they have inner defenses.

- Those who share the same (common) Spirit will stick together— *"being like-minded, having the same love, being of one accord, on one mind"* (2:2). Paul is referring to the Holy Spirit as a Uniter and not a divider. We can also extend "Spirit" to mean a good attitude toward one another because of the Holy Spirit. Attitude is a choice that an individual makes. You can choose to relate to your spouse from a negative or from a positive mindset. The kind of spirit that operates in you will show up in your outlook, and it will also affect your relationships. Couples should strive to have the same goals.

➤ Those who suffer together stay together. We learn a lot from military veterans. They have a kind of spirit of comradery that defies any circumstance in the world. Because they suffered together, they share a bonding that cuts across political lines. In the same way, Paul tells the Philippians that they are participants in the sufferings of Christ (Phil. 3:10). When families are united in their purpose, they will suffer together to achieve that purpose. Competing purposes create division.

➤ Those who have the same citizenship (commonwealth) will stick together. *"For our citizenship is in heaven . . ."* (3:20). The Philippians were Roman citizens, but Paul writes to encourage them to rise beyond their earthly status and see themselves as children of God who have a heavenly status. Many couples have endless wars arising from ethnic, racial, and tribal origins. They allow these cultural differences to interfere with their ultimate status, the heavenly status. Bickering over cultural differences saps energy out of their relationships. Imagine a soccer or football team bickering over racial differences while playing a game! Cultural differences have no place in the game. In the same way, cultural differences should not be allowed to divert attention from the couple's goals in life. What unites them is greater than their cultural differences.

➤ Those who are content whatever the circumstances will be happy in their marriage. Phil. 4:11 says, "For *I have learned in whatever state I am, to be content.*" Lack of contentment is the greatest enemy of a marital relationship. Appetite, greediness, materialism, and self-indulgence can never be fully satisfied. Materialism always takes you to another level of want. Families in the diaspora are susceptible to materialism. What they could not get in Africa, they try to get it in host countries in the diaspora. They also want to have everything within a short space of time, thereby compromising their intimacy and relationships. This is one of the reasons why families fall apart.

Ending with the reassuring words of Philippians 4:13, "I can do all things through Christ who gives me strength," serves as a powerful encouragement for every couple and family in the diaspora, emphasizing the strength found in Christ for facing life's challenges.

Works Cited

Anderson, Shane. "How to Stay Married Forever & Like It." Sermon preached at Pioneer Memorial Church, Berrien Springs, Michigan, October 14, 2023.

Application Study Bible, NIV edition. Grand Rapids, MI: Zondervan, 2005.

Ariely, Dan. "Predictably Irrational: The Hidden Forces that Shape Our Decisions." CDs read by Simon Jones.

Arnold, Bill T. *Genesis: The New Cambridge Bible Commentary.* New York: Cambridge University Press, 2009.

Bainton, Roland H. *Christendom: A Short History of Christianity and Its Impact on Western Civilization*, Vol. 1. New York: Harper & Row Publishers, 1966.

Barna, George. *Transforming Children into Spiritual Champions.* Ventura, CA: Regal Books, 2003.

Beebe, Steven A., Susan J. Beebe, Diana K. Ivy. *Communication: Principles for a Lifetime.* Boston, MA: Allyn and Bacon, 2001.

Berghahn, Daniela. *Far-Flung Families in Film: The Diasporic Family in Contemporary European Cinema.* Edinburgh: Edinburgh University Press, 2013.

Bundlender, Debbie. Ntobelang Chobokoane and Sandile Simelane, "Marriage patterns in South Africa: Methodological and substantive issues," Southern African Journal of Demography, Vol. 9, No. 1 (June 2004).

Carter, Brian. Notes from a presentation to Michiana Area Pastors, Andrews University campus, January 14, 2019.

Cloud, Henry and John Townshend. *Boundaries in Marriage.* Grand Rapids, MI: Zondervan, 1999.

Couden, Barbara, ed. *Understanding Intimate Violence.* Hagerstown, MD: Review and Herald Publishing Association, 1999.

Davison, Jean. *Gender, Lineage, and Ethnicity in Southern Africa.* Boulder, CO: Westview Press, 1999.

De Gance, "Communio: Nationwide Study on Faith & Relationships," https://communio.org.

Deridder, J. C. *The Personality of the Urban African in South Africa.* London: Routledge & Kegan Paul, 1961.

de Smedt, Johan. "Child Marriages in Rwandan Refugee Camps", Africa Journal of the International African Institute, Vol. 68, No. 2 (1998).

Dominic, C., Andrew S. Rancer, and Deanna F. Womack. *Building Communication Theory*, 3rd Ed. Prospect Heights, IL: Waveland Press, 1997.

Eberstadt, Mary. *It's Dangerous to Believe: Religious Freedom and Its Enemies.* New York: Harper, 2016.

Eisenberg, Arlene, Heidi Murkoff and Sandee Hathway. *What to expect When You are Expecting.* New York: Workman Publishing, 1996.

Eitzen, D. Stanley and Maxine Baca Zinn, *Social Problems*, 10th ed. Boston, MA: Allyn and Bacon, 2006.

Frinkel, Michael. *The Science of Sleep: Want to fall asleep? Read this story.* National Geographic (August 2018).

Goldstein, Clifford R., ed. *Adult Sabbath School Bible Study Guide, January-March.* Nampa, ID: Pacific Press, 2019.

_____. *Adult Sabbath School Bible Study Guide, April-June.* Nampa, ID: Pacific Press, 2019.

Guthrie, Tamika. "Student Movement," Andrews University (March 30, 2005).

Harari, Yuval Noah. 21 Lessons for the 21st Century. London: Penguin Random House, 2019.

Harley, Jr., Willard F. *His Needs, Her Needs.* Grand Rapids, MI: Fleming H. Revell, 2001.

_____. *Five Steps to Romantic Love.* Grand Rapids, MI: Fleming H. Revell, 2002.

_____. *Love Busters: Overcoming Habits That Destroy Romantic Love.* Grand Rapids, MI: Fleming H. Revell, 2002.

Hasel, Michael G. "My Dream for Seventh-day Adventist Education," *Adventist World* (February 2017).

Hendriksen, William. *New Testament Commentary: Galatians, Ephesians, Philippians, Colossians, and Philemon.* Grand Rapids, MI: Baker Books, 2004.

Henry, Casalnnie. *Neutralizing the Power of Fear.* Bloomington, IN: iUniverse, 2008.

Herbst, Patricia G. "The Measurement of Family Relationships," Sage Social Science Collections, 5 vols. (1), (February 1952).

Howard, Evan B. *The Brazos Introduction to Christian Spirituality*. Grand Rapids, MI: Brazos Press, 2008.

Johnson, Rick. *How to talk so your husband will listen*. Grand Rapids, MI: Revell, 2008

Jones, Alfred R., and Doris E. Jones. *A Door of Hope for the Black Family*. Pine Forge, PA: Family Outreach Publications, 1998.

Jones, Alfred R. *The Black Male's Survival Manual*. Pine Forge, PA: Family Outreach Publications, 1999.

Jones, G. Curtis. *1000 Illustrations for Preaching and Teaching*. Nashville, TN: Broadman & Holman Publishers, 1986.

Kaiser Jr, Walter C, Peter H. Davids, F. F. Bruce, Manfred T. Brauch. *Hard Sayings of the Bible*. Downers Drove, IL: InterVarsity Press, 1996.

Keil, C. F. and F. Delitzsch, *Commentary on the Old Testament, Proverbs, Ecclesiastes, Song of Solomon,* Vol. 6. Peabody, MA: Hendrickson Publishers, 2006.

Kelly, Michael. "Soul Mates," a sermon preached at Mt. Rubidoux, Riverside, CA (February 9, 2019).

Knight, George R. *Exploring Galatians and Ephesians: A Devotional Commentary*. Hagerstown, MD: Review and Herald Publishing Association, 2005.

Lahey, Benjamin B. *Psychology: An Introduction*, 9th ed. New York: McGraw-Hill, 2007.

Lander, Laura, Janie Howsare, and Marilyn Byrne, "The impact of Substance Use Disorders on Families and Children: From Theory to Practice." Department of Behavioral Medicine and Psychiatry, West Virginia University School of Medicine, Morgantown, West Virginia. Accessed online, April 30, 2023.

Levine, Janice R. and Howard J. Markman, eds. *Why do fools fall in Love?* San Francisco, CA: Jossey-Bass, 2001.

Life Application Study Bible. Grand Rapids, MI: Zondervan, 2007.

Maxwell, John C. Editor. *The Maxwell Leadership Bible.* Nashville, TN: Maxwell Motivation, Inc., 2002.

McDonald, H. D. *Forgiveness and Atonement.* Grand Rapids: Baker, 1984.

McQuilkin, Robertson and Paul Copan. An Introduction to Biblical Ethics, 3rd ed. Downers Grove, IL: InterVarsity Press, 2004.

Miller, Nicholas P. 500 Years of Protest and Liberty: From Martin Luther to Modern Civil Rights. Idaho: Pacific Press Publishing Association, 2017.

Morreale, Sherwyn P., Brian H. Spitzberg, and J. Kevin Barge. *Human Communication: Motivation, Knowledge & Skills.* Belmont, CA: Thomson Learning, 2001.

Moskala, Moskala. "Biblical-Theological Thinking: The Foundation for Transformational Ministry," an unpublished presentation at Andrews University, Berrien Springs, Michigan, October 2013.

Muller-Fahrenholz, Geiko. *The Art of Forgiveness* (Geneva: WCC Publications, 1997.

Munroe, Myles. *Myles Munroe on Relationships* (Nassau, Bahamas: Bahamas Faith Ministries International, 2008),

Myers, David G. *Psychology*, Fifth Edition (New York, NY: Worth Publishers, 1998)

Ndlovu, Herbert. "African customs and values that can enhance Seventh-day Adventists missions to South Africans with specific reference to the Zulu cultural heritage." PhD Dissertation, University of Pretoria, July 30, 2018. Consulted.

Nowlin, Arthur & Kim. *The Attitude Adjustment of the Christian Man and Woman*. Detroit, MI: Kim Logan Communications, 2004.

Olson, David, John DeFrain, and Linda Skogrand. *Marriages and Families: Intimacy, Diversity, and Strengths*. McGraw-Hill, NY: McGraw-Hill Humanities, 2004.

Onwubiko, Oliver A. *African Thought, Religion & Culture*. Enugu, Nigeria: Bigard Memorial Seminary, 1991.

Paindoctor.com, Top 10 Most Stressful Life Events: The Holmes and Rahe Stress Scale. Accessed January 1, 2019.

Peachey, Paul. *Living and Clinging: The Human Significance of the Conjugal Unions*. Lanham Seabrook, MD: The University Press of America, 2001.

Pearson, Judy C., and Paul E. Nelson. *An Introduction to Human Communication*, 8th ed. Boston: McGraw Hill, n.d.

Phillips, Bob. *42 Days to Feeling Great*. Eugene, Oregon: Harvest House Publishers, 2001.

Phiri, George Allan. *Socio-Cultural Anthropology: Christian Communication and the African Culture*. Eugene, Oregon: Resource Publications, 2009.

Pollock, David C., Ruth E. Van Reken, and Michael V. Pollock, *Third Culture Kids: Growing Up Among Worlds*. Boston, MA: Nicholas Brealey Publishing Hachette Book Company, 2017.

Pressner, Sharon J. "Pornography: Free Speech versus Civil Rights?" in Amitai Etzioni, Rights and the Common Good. New York: St. Martin's Press, 1995.

Reader, D. H. *Zulu Tribe in Transition*. Manchester: Manchester University Press, 1966.

Redmond, Mark V. *Communication: Theories and Application*. Boston, NY: Houghton Mifflin Company, 2000.

Rockey, Ron and Nancy. "Binding the Wounds," Lifestyle Renewal Institute, 2000.

Rowan, Ford. "Forgiveness and Healing in Prison," Interpretation: A Journal of Bible and Theology, Vol. 72, No. 3 (July 2018).

Ryken, Leland, James C. Wilhoit, Tremper Longmann III, eds. *Dictionary of Biblical Imagery*. Downers Grove, IL: InterVarsity Press, 1998.

Sapolsky, Robert M. *Why Zebras Don't Get Ulcers*. New York: Henry Holt Company, 2004.

Schrock-Shenk, Carolyn, ed. *Mediation and Facilitation Training Manual*. Akron, PA: Mennonite Conciliation Service, 2000.

Scott, Suzan. *Fierce Conversations*. New York: New American Library, 2002.

Seventh-day Adventist World Church. "A Statement on Transgenderism." April 11, 2017.

Shaw, Stephen J. "The Epidemic that Dare not Speak Its Name." An online interview by Jordan B. Peterson, March 2023, accessed on July 23, 2023.

Shea, William. *The Abundant Life Bible Amplifier, Daniel 7-12*, edited by George R. Knight. Boise, Idaho: Pacific Press Publishing Association, 1996.

Shorter, Aylward. *East African societies*. London: Routledge & Kegan Paul, 1974.

Smith, James. *Worried Lovers: Why do people cheat?* Posted online, September 2018.

Tawwab, Nedra Glover, *Set Boundaries, Find Peace* (New York: TarcherPerigee, 2021.

Tibbitts, Rick, with Steve Halliday. *Forgive to Live*. Nashville, TN: Integrity Publishers, 2006.

Tinarwo, Moreblessing Tandeka, and Domicic Pasura. "Negotiating and Contesting Gendered and Sexual Identities in the Zimbabwean Diaspora" (Journal of Southern African Studies, Vol. 40, No. 3, (2014).

Tobias, Kern P. "Exploring the impact of a marriage seminar on marital relationships in the Seventh-Day Adventist Church in Trinidad," D. Min. diss. Andrews University, Berrien Springs, Michigan, 2010.

Turner, Lynn H., Turner & Richard West. *Perspectives on Family Communication*, 2nd ed. Boston: McGraw Hill, 2000.

Venker, Suzanne. Will America Ever Be Ready for the Truth about Daycare? Posted online February 1, 2012. Accessed September 15, 2023.

Matthew Walker, Why We Sleep. New York: Scribner, 2017.

Weaver, Andrew J., Linda A. Revilla & Harold G. Koenig. *Counseling Families Across the Stages of Life*. Nashville, TN: Abingdon Press, 2002.

White, Ellen G. *Selected Messages*, Book 3. Washington, D.C.: Review and Herald Publishing Association, 1980.

_____. *The Adventist Home*. Hagerstown, MD: Review and Herald Publishing Association, 1952.

_____. *The Ministry of Healing*. Mountain View, CA: Pacific Press Publishing Association, 1942.

_____. *The Ministry of Healing*. Silver Springs, MD: Better Living Publications, 1990.

World Health Organization. Mental Health. 17 June 2022. Accessed online August 16, 2023.

Worthington Jr., Everett L. *A Just Forgiveness*. Downers Grove, IL: IVP, 2009.

Zeleza, Paul Tiyambe. "Rewriting the African Diaspora: Beyond the Black Atlantic," African Affairs, Vol. 104, No. 414 (Jan. 2005).

www.ingramcontent.com/pod-product-compliance
Lightning Source LLC
Chambersburg PA
CBHW071324120626

46546CB00002B/421